DEBRETT'S
GUIDE TO TRACING YOUR ANCESTRY

NOEL CURRER-BRIGGS became a full-time professional genealogist in 1953. A well-known lecturer and broadcaster in Britain and the United States, he is a Fellow of the Society of Genealogists, a founder member and former chairman of the Association of Genealogists and Record Agents and a consultant to Debrett Ancestry Research Ltd. He is the author of many books on genealogical subjects and has published numerous articles and papers in British and American historical and genealogical journals.

ROYSTON GAMBIER is a Fellow of the Society of Genealogists and of the Huguenot Society of London. He was one of the founders of the Federation of Family History Societies and the principal founder of nine British county family history societies.

Debrett's

GUIDE
TO
TRACING
YOUR
ANCESTRY

NOEL CURRER-BRIGGS AND ROYSTON GAMBIER

INTRODUCTION BY SIR IAIN MONCREIFFE OF THAT ILK, BT

FOREWORD BY IAIN SWINNERTON

HEADLINE

First published in 1981
by Webb & Bower (Publishers) Ltd

First published in paperback in 1992
by HEADLINE BOOK PUBLISHING PLC

10 9 8 7 6 5 4 3 2

ISBN 0 7472 3925 8

Typeset by
Letterpart Limited, Reigate, Surrey

Printed and bound in Great Britain by
HarperCollins Manufacturing, Glasgow

HEADLINE BOOK PUBLISHING PLC
Headline House
79 Great Titchfield Street
London W1P 7FN

Contents

Foreword

IAIN SWINNERTON

President of the Federation of the Family History Society

Genealogy as a science began in the sixteenth century and although the latter part of the nineteenth century saw the establishment of many of our present-day historical and antiquarian societies in which there was great interest in tracing and recording pedigrees, it was mainly carried out by the wealthier members of society – the aristocracy and landowning classes and the business and professional men. I suppose no one ever thought the lower classes also had pedigrees. Certainly, they obviously saw no need for anything as mundane as a society for pedigree-tracers and it was not until 1911 that the first such organization was founded. It is significant that this was called the Society of Genealogists *of London*; it was three years before it was acknowledged that interest was not confined to the capital and the territorial appellation dropped. A study of its early journals shows that the emphasis was still on royal, noble and armigerous families and this persisted for many years.

Nothing else happened on the genealogical scene for over fifty years until Dr S.W. Kingsley-Norris, a Birmingham eye surgeon and genealogical and heraldic enthusiast, decided to form a society to cover the Midland counties and so the Birmingham and Midland Society for Genealogy and Heraldry, the first in the provinces, was founded in 1963. Manchester followed suit in 1964 and over the next ten years similar societies were formed in Cheshire, Hampshire, Kent, Norfolk, Nottingham, Rossendale, Sussex and Yorkshire.

By the early 1970s, several of these were in fairly regular contact with each other and tentative links had been forged with the Society of Genealogists and the Heraldry Society. Then, at a meeting in Birmingham in June 1973, called to enlist support to bring the International Congress on Heraldry and Genealogy to this country, a quite separate resolution to found a British Federation of Genealogical, Heraldic and Allied Societies was adopted with eleven societies enrolling as founder members. This was the turning point and the dawn of the new age of the genealogy of the common man.

They were joined fairly soon, albeit somewhat reluctantly, by the Society of Genealogists and the Heraldry Society. The new Federation set out to found a society in every county in England and was helped by such television programmes as Alex Haley's 'Roots' (subsequently proved to be part fiction) and Gordon Honeycombe's search for his ancestors. Influenced by these, more and more people took up the hobby and societies sprang up all over the United Kingdom. Overseas societies (for obvious reasons mainly in the former colonies) asked to join and by the early 1980s there was a well-established network of societies throughout the English-speaking world. By 1992 the Federation of Family History Societies had 157 member societies in ten countries.

Wherever I go I am asked the same question – why have so many people suddenly taken up this pastime of tracing their ancestors and why are people so keen today on digging up the past? This applies not only to family history – historical and archaeological societies have experienced a similar growth.

I think there are several answers. Undoubtedly, sadly, there are still a few who do it for snobbish reasons in the hope that they will trace a descent from a royal or titled family or simply to be able to boast how far back they can go. Given the English system of primogeniture with younger sons having to go into (or marry) trade and some of our former sovereigns' penchants for extra-marital activities, the first is comparatively easy for many while the second is merely boring. One of the best things that has happened over the last two decades is that genealogy, the tracing of pedigrees, has been largely replaced by the study of family history. Most people now realize that researching their ancestors' occupations, hobbies and politics, as well as their virtues and vices, is so much more interesting and satisfying than merely seeing how far they can trace them back.

I would imagine most people start out of curiosity: a desire to know what sort of people their ancestors were and from whence they came. 'Total ancestry', the study of all one's ancestors, is another good thing that has come out of this new wave of interest; most people now appreciate that we inherit our physical and mental characteristics from both our paternal and maternal progenitors and only our surname from our

2

father's line. Indeed, it is unwise to rely entirely on the paternal name for our descent – as the French have it, '*La mère seulement connait le nom du père!*'

Despite this, the last twenty years have seen the birth of another quite different sort of family history society – the One-Name Society. In these, the members trace all the persons of that surname whether they are related or not. Obviously, most of these are the more unusual surnames – one would not attempt it for Smith or Jones.

I also believe that there are a large number who have taken up tracing their ancestors in a subconcious search for security. We live in a very unstable world and have become a highly mobile race, the advent of the motor car has brought freedom to travel in search of a better environment in which to live, work and educate our children. When I ask my average audience how many were born and brought up in the town or village in which they are now living, the usual answer is only about 10 per cent. The rest are strangers and we all know how the English feel about incomers. A feeling of insecurity about their place in the community can persist for some time and inevitably sets them thinking about the place from which they came and whether the family had always lived there. Experience teaches us that this is not usually the case, our ancestors were far more mobile than we like to think.

I am also asked, 'Should I join a Family History Society?' Over 90,000 people in this country alone have done so but there are many more who are still doing their own thing. The advantages of joining are many, the obvious ones being that you get a chance to meet others with the same interests and problems, and to hear speakers who are experts in different aspects of research as well as people like yourself recounting how they did it. In addition, you have access to the society's publications and genealogical aids, such as the indexes that most societies produce. Who knows, you may even meet someone researching the same family.

Whether you do or don't, this book will help you with one of the most fascinating and enjoyable hobbies there is.

Introduction

SIR IAIN MONCREIFFE OF THAT ILK, BT

Genealogy is fun. Just as a piece of furniture or a picture takes on much more interest if you know its provenance, so does an individual the more the diverse ancestral elements that went to form him or her are known. The provenance of genealogy lies within the greatest gift of all: life. True family history in depth is a tapestry of *all* those who ever lived and to whom we owe our existence, and the threads woven across it are the connected lives of their interwoven generations. Tracing it, to change the metaphor, is like a detective trying to fit together a jigsaw puzzle whose pieces have been scattered throughout the world over the centuries. It is not only natural but instructive to want to know not just the broad generalized history of the country in which you live, but the actual life-histories of the people from whom you derive your individual existence.

When you have discovered who as many as possible of your ancestors were – not merely the line of your father's surname – you will find a new thrill in learning the strange vicissitudes of their lives in diverse walks of life. Visiting the houses or places where they lived, seeking out their likenesses or their graves, handling the coins they used centuries ago – everything takes on a special interest when you know that, as it were, something of you has been there before. For families are seldom static; the rich are not always rich, nor the poor nothing but the offspring of untold centuries of poverty.

Sir Anthony Wagner, former Garter Principal King of Arms, has pointed out in *Pedigree and Progress* that it is a myth to think of social classes as distinct, self-perpetuating, hereditary corporations. On the contrary, it is easy to demonstrate that this is no more than a figment of the imagination, fostered by politicians of both Left and Right to serve their own party dogmas. Even the middle classes, whose social movement up or down was often rapid enough to be visible to the naked eye, did their best to hide this movement in the anonymity of city life.

And never forget that you each owe your very existence

not just to your parents, but to *every single one* of your personal ancestors since mankind began. It is impossible to knock out one brief link at any time in history and keep the whole chain together. Abraham Lincoln and the Aga Khan, and many more readers of these words than perhaps realize it, could never have been born had Alfred the Great's mother died in childhood.

Ponder this. None of you could ever have been born if your mother's mother's mother's mother had died in infancy. But do you know offhand who she was? It would have been no good your direct maternal great-great-grandfather marrying somebody else instead, for the child of such a marriage would have been quite different genetically from your real great-grandmother, and no descendants could ever have been *you*.

The extraordinary variety of genealogy may perhaps be illustrated by a case well known to me. The child of a Kenya settler wanted to find out about his mother's side of the family. She vaguely believed herself to be of a titled family ultimately French in origin, and her mother, a British general's daughter, believed herself to descend maternally from Admiral Bradley who had taken part in the first coastal survey of Australia and after whom Bradley Head, a landmark at Sydney in New South Wales, was named. It seemed a fairly solid Victorian background.

Admiral Bradley turned out to be a *Sergeant* Jonas Bradley who had settled in Australia and whose son had been so successful as a sheep farmer that he has an entry in the Australian *Dictionary of Biography*. Young Bradley married the daughter of an Australian explorer called Hovell; her natural brother Albert Hovell, Master Mariner of the good ship *Young Australia*, was convicted in 1869, together with two of his crew of aborigines, of murdering three persons, names unknown, on the high seas: a story reminiscent of an adventure by Joseph Conrad. The farmer Bradley's daughter married General Pearse, of the 'Fighting Fifth'; and their daughter married the natural son of a dashing Austrian count of French origin called Rességuier de Miremont, whose father sprang in the female line from industrious Pierre-Paul Riquet (1604–1680), the Baron de Bon Repos who had built the Canal du Midi from the Mediterranean to the Atlantic. The Austrian count's mother, a Hungarian countess, Amelie Festetics, belonged to what had become a very grand family (descended in the female line from Erszebet Báthory, the 'Bloody Countess' who tops the list under 'murderer' in the *Guinness Book of Records*) whose founder had been Peter Ferstetych, born before 1504, a manumitted *serf* of the Bishop of Zagreb at Sassinovec in Croatia. This then, was my mother's background, for I was that Kenya settler's son. The Midi of Languedoc, the Carpathians, the Balkans and the Australian outback alike took on a new interest for me.

It is a pity that some people seem interested only in grand descents, others only in respectable ones. Yet others seek only what is rare. I once told somebody that he descended from Charlemagne, which he hadn't known before. His only reaction was a shrug since an enormous number of other people must share in that descent. It seemed dull to me not to be excited, or at least interested, in identifying an actual flesh-and-blood forefather who lived in the eighth century, and to be able to know so much about him and even visit the chapel where he worshipped, whether he was a serf or an emperor. Indeed, quite literally, Charlemagne can be regarded as the Father of Europe; his was a most vigorous stock. If he and his third Queen, Hildegard, had never been born, no single one of his descendants would ever have been born; not George Washington, nor George III, not Hermann Goering nor Winston Churchill, not Bonnie Prince Charlie nor President Nixon. Moreover, neither could any of these people have been born if the future William the Conqueror had never been born as William the Bastard, illegitimate son of the original Harlot (Harlotte of Falaise) the tanner's attractive daughter to whose prowess in bed one single night in 1027 so many of us thus owe our very being. All our ancestors are interesting, for they were *all* necessary in handing down life to us even if they lived long, long ago.

In the quest, there are so many things that are fun too. As I have already observed, there is the discovery, if possible, of their photographs or their portraits: their iconography, as it is called. Then there are pictures of their houses or belongings. One of the oldest residences whose former occupants can still be traced is the drystone fortress of Ailech in Northern Ireland, where the ancestors of the present O'Neills of Clanaboy had their stronghold from the fifth until the eleventh century. To come to more recent times, I was shown on Lake Toba in the interior of Sumatra the ancestral stone table, stone benches and decapitation stone where cannibal feasts had been held until 1912 by the family of our hosts, the elder members of which recollected them well and described them shyly: 'But this was before we became Lutherans.'

There are so many side-lines of genealogy. I have noticed, for example, that a characteristic handwriting can sometimes be inherited as in the case of some of the Argyll family. Any study of genealogy among the early Celts requires an understanding of what social anthropologists call the 'classificatory' system, which extended among Indo-European peoples from India to Ireland, and was patrilinear. It seems probable that the Picts had a similar 'classificatory' system for purposes of succession law, but that it was matrilinear – such a system still exists among the Bemba of Zambia – which is of genealogical importance in working out the ramifications of the Pictish royal house because innumerable people now living in many countries can trace themselves back to Kenneth MacAlpin's Pictish grandmother, who was alive c AD 800. Again, heraldists seeking to disentangle relationships of heraldry should be aware that great houses often had two coats, probably one for their shield and one for their flag; the one having a device such as an eagle or a lion, the other a geometrical pattern, usually of the same colours in each case. Later branches of such families, sometimes taking different surnames in those early days, bore one of the coats alone.

However, this book is concerned with the main stream of genealogical enquiry today. It describes the sources that can be consulted, and gives an outline of the way in which you can embark upon a search of your own. I will now content myself with some introductory general observations. First, I would like to stress the universal brotherhood of Man, that all human beings belong ultimately to the same family, if only we could trace everybody down from our common source. And second, I would like to indicate the sort of lines, usually sacred or royal, through which we can trace really quite a lot of people in all walks of life today back and back into the mists of early civilization.

Einstein said 'Science without religion is lame, religion without science is blind.' And early human genealogy and religion are inextricably entwined, as I will explain. This is not perhaps the place to discuss in detail my agreement with

8

the scholastic axiom of my twenty-five times great-grand-uncle Saint Thomas Aquinas that (to quote Dr T. M. Lindsay) 'while reason and revelation are two distinct sources of truths, the truths are not contradictory: for in the last resort they rest on *one* absolute truth – they come from the one source of knowledge, God, the Absolute One'. But it has a profound bearing on the evolutionary theories of my fifth cousin four times removed – Charles Darwin – with whom I am equally in general agreement.

For nobody can fail to observe how extraordinarily the allegory of creation in the book of Genesis fits the sequence of evolution as revealed for us by the scientists. Epochs are poetically expressed as days, in much the same way as we say 'in Neanderthal Man's day'. We are told in Genesis that in the beginning 'there was light'. The scientists say that the Earth was a ball of fire. In the second epoch, as the Earth cooled, there was vapour: when the waters beneath were divided from 'the waters which were above'. Next, the waters gathered together to form seas, and the dry land appeared. Then vegetation sprang up, depending on the sunlight of the firmament for life. Next *out of the seas* came forth amphibious reptiles – 'let the waters bring forth abundantly the moving creature that hath life' – and from these reptiles evolved, notice how the order in Genesis is still correct, 'fowl' before 'beast of the earth', i.e. birds before mammals. And the last in time to be evolved was Man.

How the correct sequence of evolution was revealed to the talented Hebrews centuries before Darwin's explorations, and how much of it was known to even earlier civilizations, is beyond our present knowledge; but their poetic use of the words 'day' for 'epoch' and 'created' for 'evolved' should not obscure the wonder of it.

A moment's reflection will show that, at some single stage and in some single place, within a little family group of primates, the single anthropoid common forefather of every man living today walked this Earth. Nobody really thinks different human beings, all with ten fingers and an appendix, were separately evolved from different amoebae in separate parts of the world. The myriad coincidences would be beyond ordinary mathematical comprehension. However much other warm-blooded mammals may have branched off as our yet more remote kin at some far earlier pre-anthropoid primordial stage, 'a man's a man for a' that'. To paraphrase Kipling: we are all brothers under the skin. And to quote him: 'We be of one blood, thou and I.'

So it cannot be stressed often enough that no family is older than any other family. Some lines can be traced back further than others, but none for much more than just over a couple of millennia. Some people adopted surnames earlier than others, so that one can trace the history of an old name, especially if it is mentioned in surviving records over a long period. But I repeat for emphasis, nobody suggests that two separate human families were evolved from two different amoebae, or even from two different quadrupeds, or even from two different monkeys. If every man alive today was able to trace back the source of his Y-chromosome – the chromosome which can only be given him by his father and which alone can make him a man, and which his forefathers in turn could only have received from their forefathers – we would all find that we had each inherited our individual Y-chromosome from the very same source in the testicle of a single, joint, man-like ancestor, one individual at the anthropoid stage of evolution. That individual anthropoid's issue may have had to intermarry for generations before his distributed Y-chromosome produced men who were fully entitled to be called *Homo sapiens*, but we may nevertheless accord him the archaic name of Adam. For we all descend from him. All families spring from his. And to the age-old question, 'When Adam delved and Eve span, who was then the gentleman?' the answer is clear: Adam. How could it have been Eve? From that illustrious Y-chromosome sprang all the immemorial nobility in the world.

Throughout the world the early legends of every civilization attribute the discovery of agriculture and the arts to God-like royal ancestors. These early food producers perceived divine power in the life force which impregnated matter with energy. By concentrated prayer and ritual, part of this life force, as it were the lucky spirit of the community, was embodied in the talisman king, successor to the wise horned-priest figure of Stone Age cave paintings. Respect for sacral royalty is the earliest religion of which there is any certain knowledge. It spread with civilization throughout the world. Sacral royalty 'was the early inspiration of drama, astronomy, architecture, sculpture, painting, music, dancing, games and costume'. It also inspired the earliest ancestral records, whether oral, passed by repetition from generation to generation by bardic herald-priests, or kept by them in newly invented writing.

It is not surprising, therefore, that the earliest genealogies that have come down to us are royal ones, or those of sacred families. And since kings have tended to marry princesses and often foreign ones, throughout the centuries, it is usually through royal intermarriages over the millennia that we can trace the most ancient descent of people actually living today. Most people have royal blood; the difficulty is to trace it.

Thus nearly all the longest traceable direct male-line descents, invaluable for the tracing of the human Y-chromosomes over long periods, are those of royal or sacred houses. In Japan, for instance, the oldest great historic families go back to the imperial house itself and to priestly court nobility, all traceable since the very first written records, and already then immemorial.

When I was a Guards Officer during the Second World War, one of my comrades was Lieutenant Louis Kung, Scots Guards, *alias* K'ung Lingchieh. His parentage linked modern Chinese history with the remote past. His mother was one of the three sisters of T. V. Soong, the former Foreign Minister of China; the other two Soong sisters had married respectively Sun Yat Sen, first President of China after the overthrow of the Manchu dynasty in 1912, and Generalissimo Chiang Kai-shek. His father was Dr H. H. Kung, then Finance Minister, and I understand that they belonged to the K'ung clan who have evolved over more than seventy-five generations around the tomb of their illustrious forefather K'ung tsze, better known as the sage K'ung Fu-tze or Confucius (551–479 BC) and their genealogy had been treasured by Chinese scholars throughout two and a half millennia in their great Chia Pu or family name book. But I don't know whether any copy of this has survived the Communist 'burning of the books' throughout China. Moreover we are told that Confucius himself was a scion in the direct male line, through the dukes of Sung, of the proto-historic Shang dynasty (traditionally 1766–1121 BC). It was estimated in 1911 that some forty to fifty thousand male-line descendants of the K'ung family were living in the neighbouring city of K'iuh-fow; I would add, with possibly the oldest traceable human Y-chromosomes in the world.

In this connection, incidentally, I cannot sufficiently stress the grievous mental injustice, and the heartless blocking of all scholarly research, including medical and scientific research, caused by the operation of the Adoption Acts, even as amended by the Children Act (1975). Briefly, an adopted child, after reaching the age of eighteen, can with great difficulty obtain access to some legal information about his true parentage. The reasons for and against this are well understood. But the *descendant* of an adopted child, long after the need for concealment is dead, has no means of gaining access to the important original birth certificate of the adoptee. The unnecessary cruelty of this thoughtless ban is obvious.

To return to descents traceable over a long period, ancient dynastic families of the Caucasus have survived into the twentieth century. Some of them, such as Bagration, are traceable in the direct male line since before the Conversion of Armenia in AD 314. For these, see Cyrille Toumanoff's indispensable *Manuel de Généalogie et de Chronologie pour l'histoire de la Caucasie Chrétienne* (Rome, Edizione Aquila, 1976) to be read in conjunction with his *Studies in Christian Caucasian History* (Georgetown University Press, 1963).

Excellent examples of groping backwards through the female line by way of ancient and medieval Caucasia are to be found in Sir Anthony Wagner's *Pedigree and Progress*, already referred to, which is based primarily on Professor Prince Toumanoff's works. It contains a fascinating series of tabular pedigrees indicating 'Bridges to antiquity' whereby very many people, including once again all the present royal families of Europe, almost certainly descend, by way of crusader intermarriages with the princely houses of Armenia, from the Arsacid dynasty of Parthian monarchs such as Mithridates, who were great kings of Persia from the third century BC. This is mobility of ancestry on the grandest scale. But above all, Sir Anthony Wagner's book stresses the mobility of this ancestry between classes as well as places.

Yearning backwards to the earliest sources of identifiable ancestors, I have so far discussed mainly royal or sacred lineages, only because it is usually through them that there is the best chance of getting furthest back, following all possible lines, male or female. To recapitulate: kings marry into even older dynasties across nations, their daughters marry local nobles whose daughters in turn marry lesser landowners in their districts, and so on downwards to the farmer's younger sons' daughters who marry labourers in the villages. Thus a given Mackay clansman living in Strathnaver in the remotest north-west of Scotland in 1370 was not likely to be the ancestor of a given Robertson clansman living in Atholl in the central highlands by 1870. But King Robert II, living in 1370, had a daughter who married the Macdonald Lord of the Isles, and their daughter married the Mackay chief. As a result of local intermarriage generation after generation among the Mackay cadets in Strathnaver, there is a strong likelihood of a given clansman there in 1870 descending from King Robert II. Similarly, another of Robert II's daughters married the thane of Glamis, and in the following century Lord Glamis's daughter married the Robertson chief: again, owing to local intermarriage generation after generation among the Robertson cadets in Atholl, there is a similarly strong likelihood of a given clansman there in 1870 descending from Robert II. And from Robert II, the genealogy can of course then be carried back without difficulty into the Dark Ages. It is the royal house that is the most probable unifying factor between the two widely separated clansmen's genealogies.

Two tabular pedigrees below illustrate the way in which royal ancestry links very diverse people together across great distances in both space and time. They are selected from the very many traceable ancestors of Mr Frederick Ray Howkins, living at 21616 Kramer Avenue, St Clair Shores, Michigan, USA, whose father matriculated Arms in Lyon Register in 1968. The one shows Mr Howkins' direct male line, father-to-son, back for thirty generations over more than nine centuries. We each have of course two parents, four grandparents, eight great-grandparents, and so on backwards in time: I understand that the number of theoretical ancestors we have thirty generations back is 1,073,741,904. Since there were not that number of people in the whole wide world thirty generations ago, it follows that we are all made up of innumerable cousin marriages. But it is of extraordinary interest that, with over a thousand million (over an American billion) theoretical choices in the thirtieth generation, we can pinpoint the exact individual living in 1045 from whom this particular American citizen living today has actually inherited his Y-chromosome. Since it can only come down father to son, Mr Howkins derives his Y-chromosome from the Breton noble Alan, Seneschal of Dol before the Norman Conquest of England; from whom such historic characters as King Robert II (cited above) founder of the Stewart dynasty, the Bonnie Earl of Moray and, for that matter, Bonnie Prince Charlie, also inherited their own Y-chromosome.

The second tabular pedigree shows how, in the female line, Mr Howkins' ancient roots can be traced back over twenty-two centuries to the Parthian imperial dynasty in the third century BC; and there is good reason to believe that they in their turn linked back through other princesses to even more ancient dynasties, stretching back immemorially into the human past. At four points in this second table, the generations have been linked by dots to indicate the probable affiliation. The general affiliation, however, is not in doubt, as Khachi'k Artsruni, Prince of T'ornavan in 1042, was undoubtedly a prince of the royal house of Vaspurakan, and thus a descendant of the Bagratid princess Rhipsime who married Hamazasp II Artsruni, Prince of Vaspurakan c 800; and Samuel, Prince of the Mamikonids and heir of the Gregorid domain (slain in battle 772) was undoubtably the descendant and indeed eventual heir of the marriage of Hamazasp I, Prince of the Mamikonids (307–432) to Sahakanoysh, the Gregorid heiress. Similarly, it is certain that Vologaeses IV, the Arsacid Great King of Parthia AD 191–208, descended in the direct male line from Tiridates I, Great King 247–210 BC, son of Phriapites, son of Arsakes, but the exact relationship of each successive intermediate king of the dynasty is at present uncertain. Of the overall picture, however, there is no doubt. In both tables it has been an unexpected royal ancestor (King Charles II) who has functioned as the genealogical 'gateway to the past'. Similarly, more than three hundred thousand descendants of King Edward III of England (1312–1377) have spread his ancestral genes far and wide throughout the community and throughout the world.

Direct Male Line: Inheritance of 'Y' Chromosome
ALAN, hereditary Seneschal or Steward of Dol in Brittany, a Breton noble living *c* 1045

FLAALD, hereditary Steward of Dol (brother of Alan, one of the leaders of the First Crusade 1097)
|

ALAN fitz Flaald, feudal Baron of Oswestry, Sheriff of Shropshire on the Welsh border 1101
|

WALTER fitz Alan, 1st Great Steward of Scotland, granted great estates by King David I, and died 1177
|

ALAN fitz Walter, 2nd Great Steward of Scotland, a Crusader with Richard Coeur-de-Lion
|

WALTER, 3rd Great Steward of Scotland, first to take the surname of Stewart, died 1241
|

ALEXANDER, 4th Great Steward of Scotland, co-Regent of Scotland died 1283
|

Sir JOHN Stewart of Bonkyl, 'whose bravery Wallace praised above all men', killed at Falkirk 1298
|

Sir ALAN Stewart of Dreghorn, killed at the battle of Halidon Hill 1333
|

Sir ALEXANDER Stewart of Darnley, feudal Baron of Darnley 1371
|

Sir ALEXANDER Stewart of Darnley, feudal Baron of Darnley, d. *c* 1404
|

Sir JOHN Stuart of Darnley, Seigneur d'Aubigny and Count of Evreux, killed commanding the Scots in France 1421
|

Sir ALAN Stuart of Darnley, Seigneur d'Aubigny, murdered in a feud with the Boyds 1439
|

JOHN, 10th Earl of Lennox (by descent from its heiress) 1495
|

MATTHEW, 11th Earl of Lennox, killed at the battle of Flodden 1513
|

JOHN, 12th Earl of Lennox, captured and murdered by the Hamiltons at the battle of Manuel 1526
|

MATTHEW, 13th Earl of Lennox, Regent of Scotland, mortally wounded by the Hamiltons 1571
|

HENRY, King Consort of Scots (married Mary Queen of Scots), previously Lord Darnley, assassinated 1563
|

JAMES I, King of Great Britain, united the Crowns of England and Scotland, 1625
|

CHARLES I, King of Great Britain, beheaded 1649
|

CHARLES II, King of Great Britain 1685

CHARLES, 1st Duke of Richmond & Lennox, Duc d'Aubigny (natural son) 1723

CHARLES, 2nd Duke of Richmond & Lennox, Duc d'Aubigny 1750

WILLIAM Howkins, born 1747 (natural son) farmer and carpenter

JOHN Howkins, contractor, born 1782

JOHN Howkins, civil engineer, born 1807

JOSEPH Howkins, coppersmith, born 1827

JOHN BARTHOLOMEW Howkins, coppersmith, born 1847

JOHN BARTHOLOMEW Howkins, electrical contractor, born 1889

JOHN DELMARE Howkins, born in Ontario 1920, resident in Michigan USA

FREDERICK RAY Howkins, citizen of the USA, born 1948

Descent through the female line
Arsakes Vologaeses IV Dikaios Epiphanes Philhellen, Great King or Shah of Persia AD 191–208 (36th Great King of the Parthian imperial dynasty founded in 249 BC)

Chosroes I, King of Armenia AD 191–216, maintained the old pagan fire-altars

Tiridates II, King of Armenia 216–252, still a pagan Zoroastrian

Chosroes II, the Valiant, King of Western Armenia, slain by his brothers in 297

Tiren (Helios) Tiridates IV, first Christian King of Armenia 298–350

Chosroes III, King of Armenia 330–339

Bambishn of Armenia (married Athenoganes, son of Hesychius, Primate of Armenia 342–348)

Saint Narses the Great, hereditary Bishop and Primate of Armenia 355–373

Saint Isaac the Great, hereditary Bishop and Primate of Armenia 378–438

Sahakanoysh, the Gregorid heiress (m. Hamazasp I, Prince of the Mamikonids 387–432)

INTRODUCTION

Hamazaspian, Mamikonid prince (brother of Saint Vardan and Saint Hmaycak)

Hmaycek, Mamikonid prince

Mushel, Mamikonid prince, 555

David, Mamikonid prince, *c* 600

Hamazasp II, Prince of the Mamikonids and heir of the Gregorid domain, Prince of Armenia 655–658

Hrahat, Mamikonid prince

David, Mamikonid prince, d. 744 (brother of Gregory I, Prince of the Mamikonids)

Samuel, Prince of the Mamikonids, heir of the Gregorid domain, killed 772

Mamikonid princess (m. Smbat VI, Prince of the Bagratids, Constable of Armenia for the Caliph, k. 772)

Ashot the Carnivorous, Prince of Armenia 806–926

Rhipsime, Bagratid princess (m. Hamazasp II Artsruni, Prince of Vaspurakan *c* 800)

Ashot I Abulabus Artsruni, Prince of Vaspurakan 836–874

Grigor Derenik Artsruni, Prince of Vaspurakan 857–868 and 874–886

Gagik III Artsruni, Prince (908) then King of Vaspurakan 943

Ahusahl Hamazasp III Artsruni, King of Vaspurakan 958–968

Derenik, Artsrunid prince (brother of Sennecherib John Artsruni, King of Vaspurakan 1003–1021

Khachi'k Artsruni, Prince of T'ornavan 1042

Hasan, Artsrunid prince, eleventh century

Abulgherib Artsruni, Byzantine Governor of Tarsus

Artsrunid princess (m. Oshim I, Prince of Lambron *c* 1071–1110, Sebastus)

Hetum II, Prince of Lambron and Tarsus 1110–1143, Sebastus)

Oshin II, Prince of Lambron 1143–1170, Sebastus

INTRODUCTION

Hetum III, Prince of Lambron 1170–1200 d. 1218

Constantine the Thagadir, Prince of Lambron 1220–1249

Hetum IV, lord of Lambron, died 1250

Alice of Lambron (m. the Crusader baron Balian d'Ibelin, Seneschal of Cyprus, died 1302)

Guy d'Ibelin, Seneschal of Cyprus, 1309

Alice d'Ibelin (m. Hugh IV de Lusignan, King of Cyprus 1324–1358 titular King of Jerusalem)

James de Lusignan, King of Cyprus 1382–1398, titular King of Armenia

Janus de Lusignan, King of Cyprus 1398–1432

Anne de Lusignan, princess of Cyprus (m. Louis, Duke of Savoy 1468)

Margaret of Savoy (m. Pierre de Luxembourg, Count of Saint Pol, who died 1482)

Marie de Luxembourg, Countess of Saint Pol, died 1546 (m. François Count of Vendôme)

Charles de Bourbon, Duke of Vendôme, died 1537

Antoine de Bourbon, King Consort of Navarre, Duke of Vendôme, died 1562

Henri IV, King of France and Navarre, assassinated 1610

Princess Henrietta Maria of France (m. Charles I, King of Great Britain, beheaded 1649)

Charles II, King of Great Britain, died 1685

Charles, Duke of Richmond & Lennox, KG (natural son, by Louise de Kéroalle, Duchess of Portsmouth)

Charles, Duke of Richmond & Lennox, KG died 1750

William Howkins (natural son, by Sophie Howkins), farmer and carpenter, born 1747

John Howkins, contractor, born 1782

John Howkins, civil engineer, born 1807

Joseph Howkins, coppersmith, born 1827

John Bartholomew Howkins, coppersmith, born 1847

John Bartholomew Howkins, electrical contractor, born 1889

John Delmare Howkins, born in Ontario 1920, resident at St Clair Shores, Michigan

Frederick Ray Howkins, citizen of the United States of America, born 1948

Ancient Roots

Finally, there is the question as to which are the oldest traceable native American descendants. Many noteworthy people including modern Europe's great benefactor General Marshall of the Marshall Plan have sprung from the marriage of the colonist John Rolfe and the famous Virginian princess, Pocahontas (1595–1619), daughter of Powhatan, king of all the redskin tribes from the Alleghenies to the Atlantic seaboard. There are also the Spanish dukes of Moctezuma, descended from the maternal grandson of Halco Hucpantzin (Don Pedro of Moctezuma), son of the celebrated Montezuma, actually Moteuczoma II, Emperor of Mexico, who perished in 1520; and whose ancestry, we are given to understand in Stokvis' *Manuel d'Histoire, de Généalogie et de Chronologie* (Leyden, 1888), was traceable through twelve further generations by way of the Aztec king Acamapechtli of Tenochtitlan (1350–1404) back to the Toltec king Totepeuh II (985–1026). By a happy combination of the proud native and the conquistador, the then Conde de Moctezuma was Spanish Viceroy of Mexico 1696–1701. It is to be hoped that as many other people as possible who have any redskin ancestry will record as much of it as is known while there is yet time.

We should all set to and emulate the effort behind Alex Haley's remarkable *Roots*, where he may have been misled about the exact village in Africa but nevertheless tracked down his American slave ancestry across the wide Atlantic to the aristocratic Mandinka kindred who bore the surname of Kinte in the former kingdom of Baddibu on the Gambia. And Mandinka history in general is known for the last thousand years, though it is rather an irony that although they abolished cannibalism throughout their conquests in West Africa they were themselves famous as slave-traders. Apart from the records kept in the Moslem and Christian north, such as those of the sultans of Morocco and the former imperial dynasty of Ethiopia, most black African genealogies are oral (as in Polynesia), but none the less valuable for all that, as their keeping was a sacred task. Thus the forefathers of the present Sabataka of the Baganda, son of my late friend 'King Freddie', the last Kabaka of Buganda, at whose ancestral court some of the ritual ceremonies went back to Ancient Egypt, are known through some thirty-five generations back to prince Kintu, the first Kabaka about 1300, an incoming royalty from a neighbouring kingdom whose dynasty is believed to have come by way of Abyssinia. In Africa, we may have come full circle, back to the cradle of Mankind.

In this introduction I have led you from the beginning of humankind up to some of the earliest traceable sources of present-day individual genealogy. This book takes over and leads you onwards from there.

CHAPTER ONE
Family History
Yesterday and Today

Not for many centuries has the family as an institution been under such heavy and sustained attack as it is today, and nowhere is loneliness and the sense of rootlessness more complete than in modern cities. Twentieth-century urban civilization threatens family life in much the same way that traditional Roman values and family traditions were destroyed during the early years of the Empire. Since Western European civilization owes as much to Rome, and especially to Roman ideals of family life, as to the Jews, we should, perhaps begin by examining the role of the family in these two cultures.

The religion of ancient Rome was first and foremost the religion of the family. The very word religion means binding together. By extension, this religion of the family became the religion of the state. The central concept of Roman religion was the idea of genius, which begins from the paterfamilias who, in begetting children, becomes the head of a family. His essential character was isolated and given a separate spirit-existence; he carried on the family which owed to him its continuity and looked to him for protection. Thus, as a link in that mysterious chain of father-son-father-son, each individual gained new significance, setting him against a background which, instead of being a continuous surface, was broken up in such a way that one of its pieces became himself. His genius, therefore, was that which placed him in a special relationship to his long-dead forebears and to those of his progeny as yet unborn. Genius was thought of as a chain of mysterious power, linking the family from one generation to another; and it was because of this that the Roman father could see himself as a link in this unseen chain.

The traditional function of the family in Jewish culture was to propagate the race, and the family itself was a close-knit one in which the home was – and still to a large extent is – regarded as the basic religious institution, in which the individual found the completion not only of his personality, but also of his highest personal fulfilment in marriage and the continuation of the larger family. Whereas in Roman society the veneration of one's ancestors was due on account of the example they had set and so was of paramount importance, in Jewish society, especially of the Diaspora, children were the chief concern of their parents, because through them the hope of Jewish survival in a hostile world could be kept alive.

Greek attitudes to family life and to marriage differed markedly from Roman and Jewish attitudes. In Classical times neither married nor unmarried women were regarded as legally entitled to act independently. They remained subject all their lives to the authority of a male citizen, usually their father or husband, but in the absence of either, to a male tutor or near relative. In Periclean Athens women who had been born free had no more political or legal rights than slaves. Their position contrasted strikingly with that of women under the Minoan and Achaean civilizations, who although not considered the equals of men did enjoy much more liberty than they would have been allowed at Athens. Such was the threat of misogyny in ancient Greece that strict laws were passed against celibacy. At Athens, while not prohibited officially, celibacy was, nonetheless, uncongenial to the custom of the country. The desire to have at least one son led most young men to marry sooner or later, though marriage, more often than not, was for convenience or for the promotion of business interests. In fifth-century Athens, at least, wives hardly ever saw their husbands, except in bed. The couple rarely ate together, unless a family reunion took place; children were educated outside the home, the boys in the gymnasia and the girls in the gynecea. Christianity rejected most of what it found in Greek family life, but blended with the Roman reverence for ancestral custom and standards of public duty the Jewish concept of the family, wherein God was seen as the Father of all mankind, who to show His love for His earthly children had sent His Son to teach them that all men were brothers and members of one family, the Church. By the nineteenth century it would be hard to say which element was the more dominant.

There are few who lack all curiosity about their forefathers and nowhere is this truer than among those who have been adopted or brought up without any knowledge of their parentage. It is the natural human instinct to speculate upon one's ancestors – where they lived and what they did – and it is not surprising that ancestral records and genealogies can be found in the earliest records of civilized man. The application of genealogical techniques to the study of genetics and hereditary characteristics from diseases to handwriting will be considered elsewhere, and this application is increasing as the efficiency of method and of diagnosis improves. The actuarial evaluation of risks in the insurance industry, accident proneness, health potential, longevity and even criminal and anti-social tendencies all appear to be inherited either genetically, or because of family, economic and environmental considerations; the study of all these can be enriched by family history, for while much of human behaviour is governed by environment, heredity plays an equal, if not more important part.

The study of family history is relevant to the laws governing inheritance and intestacy. Peculiarities of custom for succession at various times and in various countries require accurate knowledge of family if correct descent is to be legally established. Lawyers, therefore, have need of the skill of genealogists in such circumstances. Sociology, economics, the study of population movement, demography and the compatibility of groups of different ethnic origin, likewise depend upon it. For example, a study of the effect upon Kentish coalmining families of the immigration of miners from Durham and Wales early in the present century showed that there was considerable friction due to differences in local customs, speech, culture and behaviour. Although there was integration by marriage, such marriages were never secure, and the consequently disrupted families may well have been a direct cause of a very high rate of delinquency found among their children.

As has already been mentioned, there are strong forces striving to undermine the family and the hereditary system. George Orwell points out in *Nineteen Eighty-four* that 'class privilege' against which Marxists are trained to fight is based upon the false assumption that what is not hereditary cannot be permanent. That hereditary aristocracies have always been short lived is overlooked, whereas adoptive organizations such as the Roman Catholic Church have sometimes lasted for hundreds or thousands of years. The essence of oligarchical rule, he rightly points out, is not father-to-son inheritance but the persistence of a certain world-view imposed by the dead upon the living. A ruling group is a ruling group, so long as it can nominate its successors. Marxists are not concerned with perpetuating their blood but with perpetuating their political system. *Who* wields power is unimportant, provided the hierarchical structure remains the same.

In the same way, a deeper knowledge of history, and especially family history, makes it harder for the Party to fool the people. Past events, as Orwell rightly said, have no objective existence, but survive in written records and human memory. An oligarchy in full control of the records can falsify history at will. Thus the more an interest in family history is encouraged the more people will understand the truth of history, and the less they are likely to be taken in by ignorant political claptrap.

The present attack on the family may not always be motivated by sinister political ends, for it would be grossly unjust to accuse those who seek easier divorce and abortion of wishing to destroy the family as an institution. But the danger is real, and people should be made aware of it.

The fact remains that those who lived in closely-knit communities, whether they were isolated, rural peasant villages or Jewish, shtetl communities, knew more about true equality and worried less about class differences than their modern urban descendants.

The threat to Jewish family life in the United States and Western Europe is somewhat different from that which faces Christians. In his study of Jewish family life in the United States, Judson T. Landis found that the percentages of divorced and separated parents were 3.3 per cent for the Jews, 7.7 per cent for Roman Catholics and 10 per cent for Protestants, and for those of no religious faith it was 18.2 per cent. But while until recently Jewish families were more closely knit than those of other faiths or none, and probably still are, nevertheless, in recent years the rate of intermarriage between Jews and Gentiles has greatly increased. This tendency, while it must be welcomed on one level as a sign that the Jewish minority is becoming assimilated into the majority culture, at the same time poses a threat to the traditional Jewish family values and, should persecution return, to the ability of the Jewish way of life to survive. In

1963 Erich Rosenthal published a study of intermarriage in the Washington DC area in the *American Jewish Year Book*, which showed that while the overall ratio of Jewish intermarriage was reasonably small, the actual rate among the younger generation, namely those actually marrying at the time, was very much higher. Intermarriage has since become a burning topic for American Jewry, but there is unanimous agreement that intermarriage is growing, will continue to grow, and represents a great danger to the future of the Jewish community.

Writing in *Enemies of Society* (London, 1977), Paul Johnson made much of the need to use words correctly, describing it as one of the most important elements in precision of thought. Skill in thinking logically and precisely is what we mean by science. This criterion is equally applicable to the science of genealogy: unless the truth is precisely sought and revealed, genealogies are no better than myths or fairy-tales. Genealogy has only recently emerged from a period of unscientific abuse during which it pandered to the conceit of those who indulged in it. This undoubtedly contributed to the erroneous yet trendy belief that the British are living in an ossified, class-ridden society. Indeed, the Marxist doctrine of the class struggle, so far as British society is concerned, is based on an almost complete ignorance of the historical and genealogical facts.

The science of genealogy must therefore be based on objectively established foundations using rational methods and mature criteria of proof. Great as his achievement was in tracing his ancestry to West Africa, this is where Alex Haley, the author of *Roots* finally fails. The work of historical demographers, especially of men like Laslett and Wrigley in England or Ganiage and Goubert in France, has shown scientifically how the classes in Western European society are constantly changing and that these changes are no new phenomenon of the twentieth-century reformers nor the result of a particular economic or social dogma. This is not to deny the existence of tensions between groups of people with different social and economic interests and backgrounds, which are both inevitable and desirable for progress. The concept of the class struggle and the perpetuation of the myth that people with a certain background or education behave in a certain exclusive and anti-social manner against the interests of the working class (whatever that term may mean) are good examples of pseudo-scientific half-truths. Both notions are based on premises which are largely untrue and almost totally illusory. Historians and sociologists have, to be sure, written about the rise of the middle classes and the decline of the aristocracy and so on, but what in fact they have done is to draw general conclusions from a few examples of individuals and their families who had the ability to influence national and international events, and who experienced economic success or failure on an exceptional scale. The power and affluence of the Cecils, Rothschilds or Wedgwoods were only marginally shared by the whole social class to which they belonged. Their success (or failure) was due to the ability and intelligence of a few individuals. If by assortative mating these families were able to retain their power and affluence for several generations, this was because the social conditions in which they lived enabled them to do so. If, however, we go back to before the Reformation, we find just as many or just as few examples of men of humble origin attaining great power and wealth: Wolsey and Becket to name but two. Had it not been for the Church's rule of celibacy, no doubt they too would have founded influential families.

The Need for Family History
The need for genealogy arose from people's curiosity about their origins. For a long time legends were enough, but genealogy is the purest form of history as it concerns individuals, and, eventually, the desire to find the objective truth concerning the actual ancestors was to exert itself. The personification of history, which was the original purpose of genealogy, is still its greatest fascination, all the more so now that it is (or should be) dealing in scientifically proven facts. Tracing the history of one family is an admirable way of learning history. The reflection of wars and great national events on a set of individual families can sometimes tell one much more than the wide-ranging generalizations of a theorizing politico-economic historian; similarly how much deeper an understanding of social history can be derived by reading the plain facts about families without having them interpreted and analysed by a sociologist, incapable of thinking in anything but twentieth-century terms.

The twisting of facts to achieve a more pleasing result in a pedigree is as old as genealogy itself and still, regrettably, not unknown today. The biblical genealogies came to be dominated by the idea of purity of descent, illustrating the continuity of the race in exile. The first records in Greece were genealogical by nature, but open to abuse and of little historical value. Before the Roman Empire collapsed, the falsifying of patrician pedigrees back to Aeneas was a noted feature of that civilization. Busts of bogus ancestors would be placed in the shrines rather in the way that latter-day parvenus purchased their family portraits in antique shops.

The growth of genealogy took place as nations established themselves with modes of government and legal systems. Royal genealogies, as set out in the chronicle books, were obviously of the utmost importance in deciding the succession of kings and princes. The desire to assert the privileges of an aristocracy by birth was a powerful factor in Roman and Greek times (even in the days of the Republic) and in the development of genealogy throughout modern history. Inheritance is the heart of the hereditary principle and to settle disputes as to the inheritance of property, particularly real estate, genealogy came into its own.

The sixteenth century saw the start of collections of genealogies in manuscript and printed volumes; and the scholarship of the antiquaries of the seventeenth century uncovered material of immense value to the genealogist and demographer. Dugdale's prototype *County History of Warwickshire* and the work of the versatile Gregory King, the father of population studies, are outstanding examples of this period. Dugdale was also the first to produce, in his *Baronage*, a decent collection of the pedigrees of titled families. The eighteenth-century aristocratic view of genealogy is best summed up by Lord Chesterfield, commissioning, in a sarcastic gesture, portraits of Adam and Eve de Stanhope; and it was not until the nineteenth century that the pride of *Peerages* grew to such remarkable proportions. The 1700s had seen the appearance of *Collins's Peerage*, a largely legendary work which was corrected quite reasonably by Sir Egerton Brydges in its fifth edition (1778), apart from the insertion of his own forged ancestry. This is a characteristic syndrome of genealogists who, though reliable on other people's pedigrees, often get so hooked up on their own family trees that they alter records to suit their delusions of grandeur.

The nineteenth century was the golden age of bad genealogy; a whole shoddy industry, propped up by the pretensions of the parvenus to social status, supplied bogus evidence of gentility. There was also the craving for medieval romanticism, and to satisfy the families (the customers) some lamentable exercises in 'Gothick phantasie' were perpetrated. Mythological twaddle was put into the beginning of the pedigrees, which would often begin with the dread phrase 'The origins of this ancient family are lost in the mists of antiquity . . .'; whereas it was often more likely – social mobility being one of the key factors in tracing a genealogy – that the origins were lost in the dust thrown up by their carriage wheels. Genealogy became almost irredeemably tainted with the stigma of snobbery.

The twentieth century has been the age of the genealogy of the common man. Everyone has ancestors, and to a genealogist the fourteen generations behind Harold Wilson are of as much interest as those of the 14th Earl of Home. The Society of Genealogists was founded in 1911 to promote interest among amateur family historians; in 1968 the first professional body (the Association of Genealogists and Record Agents) was formed to establish codes of practice. During the 1970s the number of family history societies and One-Name family associations in Great Britain has risen from two or three to well over 150, and the same increase in interest and activity is to be found throughout the English-speaking world.

CHAPTER TWO
Genealogy and Genetics

From the earliest times heredity was regarded as the most important factor in deciding a child's future. The reason for this was the observation that children often resemble their parents, and that brothers and sisters often resemble each other. This is particularly obvious in the case of identical twins, who are not only identical with respect to heredity, but also very similar indeed in their respective personalities and talents. Thus the study of heredity is closely linked with that of family history.

This way of looking at the origins of personality was supported by the fact that certain types of ability run in families. One has only to think of the Bach, Russell or Cecil families or the descendants of Josiah Wedgwood and Charles Darwin. But it is not at all clear why family resemblances should be interpreted in terms of heredity rather than environment. It is, indeed, possible that the outstanding qualities of the Bachs, Darwins, Cecils and Russells may have been transmitted through the exceptionally favourable environment the parents provided for their children and grandchildren. Conversely, the fate of children with feeble-minded parents may just as easily be explained in terms of unfavourable environment. It is clearly impossible to argue from the resemblance of children to their parents to the importance of either heredity or environment, simply because both these hypothetical causes would work in the same direction.

Studies of inheritance have revealed a phenomenon known as 'regression to the mean'. The children of exceptionally tall parents will be tall, but not quite so tall as their parents. The same applies to children with very short parents who will tend to be somewhat taller than their parents, though still below average height. This phenomenon is quite universal and has been found to obtain, not only in relation to physical characteristics, but mental ones as well, and intelligence, in particular, has been studied exhaustively in this respect. The children of very bright and very dull parents respectively regress to the mean. This regression also obtains in the field

29

of personality, so that the children of exceptionally unstable or of extroverted parents will be more stable and more introverted than their parents.

The truth is that genetic factors may produce dissimilarities just as readily as similarities. Each time a man and a woman beget a child, their genes are mingled in such a way as to produce a new and different combination which ensures that each individual is completely different from any other. Only identical twins have identical heredity. Brothers and sisters may be, and usually are, like each other, and may resemble their parents in some respects, but we can all point to people who are very unlike their parents and siblings. This is what would be predicted from our knowledge of the segregation of genes, and it is this dissimilarity that probably forms the strongest reason for asserting the importance of genetic factors. On the environmental hypothesis, brothers and sisters should be much more like each other than they usually are, especially if they have all enjoyed the same kind of home environment and upbringing. Environmental factors alone would not account for the very great dissimilarities often found between siblings who have been brought up together. Thus heredity produces both similarities as well as dissimilarities, and it is important to remember this when looking back on one's own family history.

It has often been asked how familial data can be used to substantiate the claim that heredity plays an important part in causing individual differences in intelligence. A knowledge of the degree of consanguinity between different types of kin makes it possible to deduce the precise amount of similarity that ought to be observable between them with respect to intelligence. Thus the highest degree of relationship should be found for identical twins; that between fathers or mothers on the one hand, and sons or daughters on the other, should be about half that seen for identical twins. The relationship between uncles and nephews, aunts and nieces should be smaller again, and so on. If genetic factors alone were the ones that were active, the degree of similarity should coincide with the degree of relationship. When this is done, observation comes close to theory, indicating that the effect of environment is not very strong. After all, the different members of a family enjoy broadly the same environment, yet the dissimilarities in IQ between them increase significantly the lower the degree of consanguinity.

Similar studies have been carried out with personality, in which identical and fraternal twins have been studied, and the outcome has usually been much the same. On the whole, genetic factors exert a powerful influence on the different aspects of personality and usually exceed that of environment, although the precise values depend upon the particular personality traits examined. The most convincing evidence for strong genetic determination is found in people's tendency to be sociable, impulsive and generally extrovert, as opposed to the contrary traits. Almost equally good evidence is available for emotional instability as opposed to sang-froid.

Another way of studying heredity and environment is by looking at the characters of adopted children. Those adopted in the first few months of life owe their biological inheritance to their true parents, but their environment is provided exclusively by their adoptive parents. The question arises whether they resemble their true parents more than their adoptive ones. The answer is simple. Adopted children are more like their true parents in intelligence and do not resemble their adoptive parents to any notable extent. This often leads to adoptive parents being disappointed, for they hope that by providing a good environment, they will be able to bring up their adopted children to the level of their own. Of course, they may be lucky, and find they have adopted a genius, but the bright child may be held back if the adoptive parents are dull or intellectually much inferior.

The inheritance of intelligence can be studied in the offspring of inbred families. Some genes are dominant, others recessive. Intelligence, being obviously useful, is likely to show dominance in its mode of inheritance. If any kind of inbreeding takes place, the children of such marriages will show an increase of dominant characteristics, some of which may be desirable while others are undesirable.

An equally important consideration relates to the question of assortative mating. In other words, birds of a feather tend to flock together: intelligent men tend to marry intelligent women. This powerfully increases the heritability of this particular characteristic. However, no such assortative mating can be demonstrated in the field of personality. Extroverts do not tend to marry extroverts more often than introverts; emotionally unstable people do not tend to choose neurotic partners more often than stable ones.

Given all these facts, genealogical investigations of single families, while having little or no scientific importance as such, can be all the more fascinating for the investigator who tries to discern in the pattern of family history the differing threads of heredity and environment. In individual cases these can never be conclusively demonstrated to be responsible for a particular characteristic, but we can reasonably argue from what is known about genetics to the individual case, and arrive at some plausible hypothesis about what, in our own make-up, we owe to our ancestors through the agency of genetics, and what through the agency of environment.

Graphology and Personality

More often than not the only 'artefacts' a person leaves for posterity which have emanated from him personally and are in essence uniquely 'of him' are his handwritten records. Handwriting is a record of the individual expression of his personality, and can be studied in detail if it appears in diaries and letters, and any changes over the years can be observed. A handwriting consultant with good historical background and knowledge, who understands the milieu and the copy-books of the time, can build up a picture of someone who died hundreds of years ago. For example, the disturbed writing of King James I and the writing of the ill-fated King Charles I of the United Kingdom brings their personalities to life in relation to the way they affected the course of history.

The study of human personality from handwriting is called graphology. An interest in the connection between handwriting and personality recurs throughout history. Aristotle and the Roman historian Suetonius Tranquillus are quoted as having shown interest in the subject, the latter in *The Lives of the Caesars*. John Keats said in a letter, 'I am convinced more and more day by day that fine writing is next to fine doing, the top thing in the world.' Disraeli, Goethe, Robert Browning and Baudelaire all flirted with the subject, which was intermittently a fashionable intellectual pursuit in Europe at the time. Sir Walter Scott obviously had serious thoughts on the matter as can be seen in this quotation from *Chronicles of Canongate*:

Nay, my first impression was to thrust it into the fire . . . a little reflection made me ashamed of this feeling of impatience, and as I looked at the even, concise yet tremulous hand in which the manuscript was written, I could not help thinking, according to an opinion I have heard seriously maintained, that something of a man's character may be conjectured from his handwriting. That neat, but crowded and constrained, small hand argued a man of a good conscience, well-regulated passions, and, to use his own phrase, an upright walk in life, but it also indicated narrowness of spirit, inveterate prejudice, and hinted at some degree of intolerance, which though not natural to the disposition, had arisen out of a limited education. The passages from Scripture and the classics, rather profanely than happily introduced, and written in a half-text character to mark their importance, illustrated that peculiar sort of pedantry which always considers the argument as gained if secured by a quotation.

Around 1840, a pioneer movement interested in the subject developed in France as a result of the studies of the Abbé Flandrin and the Abbé Jean-Hippolyte Michon; the latter spent many years of his life making a dossier of handwriting and the personality quirks of the writers. He coined the word 'graphology' and after the publication of his books *Les mystères de l'écriture* and *La methode pratique de graphologie* there was a great deal of interest in the subject in France.

With the end of the nineteenth century, the focal point of interest in graphology moved from France to Germany. Dr Ludwig Klages, who had already published several works on philosophy, wrote five books on graphology and became the leading force in Germany on the matter. Now in the second half of the twentieth century handwriting analysis is, and has been for many years, accepted in Germany as a valid subject for scientific study and as a commonplace tool for use in the business of personnel selection and vocational guidance.

Graphology is thus a science and an art. Handwriting is fixed and can be measured and it is possible to classify it in terms of size, proportions and angles with reference to age, sex and profession. But handwriting analysts have to draw up their reports in words, and it is often difficult to transpose scientific data into clear, concise language. Herein lies the art of interpreting handwriting, and it is because some analysts lack the gift of clearly expressing what the analysis of the writing tells them, that the subject has so often been led into disrepute.

The roots of our writing today can be found in early cave paintings and drawings. A picture that tells a story is called a pictograph, many examples of which survive among primitive peoples to this day. American Indian culture is particularly rich in the number of surviving pictographic documents. But it is important to understand that pictographs were visual images in no way connected to speech or language. Pictures and symbols, in time, came to stand for ideas and also became associated with sounds and syllables. Eventually individual alphabets developed with a sign representing each sound. Ironically the pictorial symbol has now reappeared for traffic signs, etc., and is universally understood bridging national languages and drawing people together.

Handwriting fashions change like those of costume and architecture. They are shaped by the social climate and changes in taste reflecting the spirit of the times and also by the technology of the day and materials available. When paper was scarce and expensive it was cheaper to write with a stick in damp clay; when feathers were made into pens and the art of turning skins into vellum was discovered the style changed again. The ball-point pen has similarly changed modern writing radically. The thick, rounded letter-forms of the Carolingian hand which developed in France in the early Middle Ages changed imperceptibly into a more angular Gothic style at about the same time that round arches gave way to pointed ones in ecclesiastical and military architecture. Gothic, in turn, gave way during the Renaissance to a more flowing and graceful style influenced, no doubt, by the severe simplicity of the classical architectural forms which inspired the new movement. It is perhaps not insignificant that the Germans had a preference for the disciplined, iron-hard Gothic script right up to the time of Hitler.

In England a number of different 'hands' emerged around the middle of the sixteenth century. There was a native plain hand for correspondence, secretary hand and italic script for formal documents such as wills and parish registers, and court hand for legal documents, especially those written in Latin.

With the invention of the steel nib at the end of the

seventeenth century, commerce and the law adopted copper-plate script which endured to the end of the nineteenth century and beyond. The early twentieth century saw the introduction of school copy-books written in a flowing, connected style with a rightward-moving slant and tall uppers with a confident look about them. This style admirably reflected the optimistic materialism, integrity and dedication of the great Empire-builders. Following the catastrophe of the First World War there was another significant change in writing style with the emergence of 'print script', an upright, disconnected and rounded style which did not lend itself to cursive elegance. Its introduction into the class-room was to herald the arrival of our uncertain modern age and of the utilitarian ball-point pen. In women's fashions it was the age of the short skirt and 'separates' which took over from matching suits. In the world of art it was the age of abstract cubism, surrealism, dada and ultimately nihilism; in architecture it was the age of By-pass Variegated, Stockbroker's Tudor and Gaumount-British Glossy.

Today people write smaller than they did a century ago. Personalities tend to be smaller because they tend to specialize. In fashion both men and women favour jeans, and captions on films are often written without capital letters. Victorian corsets have been consigned to the flames along with bras, and handwriting, like architecture has lost its beauty in the cult of punk, lack of delight and overwhelming cynicism.

In the West we write from left to right, so in the field of handwriting the future, where we are going to, is on the right, the past, where we have come from on the left. Lack of discipline and a sense of purpose for the future is reflected in a notable increase in 'left' tendencies, an increase in left-handedness and backward (or leftward) sloping writing. People are more concerned with the past and what has gone before; this is epitomized by the great popularity of historical spectaculars and what has loosely been called the nostalgia business. If we think of paternalism as being associated with the right (not necessarily in the political sense, of course), then maternalism can be associated with the left. It is significant, therefore, that we live in the age of the first British woman Prime Minister and of women's lib.

It can be seen that in families where correspondence and

diaries have been kept, graphological examination of these documents can shed considerable light upon the characters of the people who wrote them.

Here is an example. Several dozen samples of writing covering five generations of a family were subjected to minute examination, in particular that of George, and his wife, Jane, and their son Simon. Simon was born when his two grandfathers were very old men, and he died before most of his grandchildren were born. Nevertheless it was possible to trace through these five generations certain characteristics. In the case of George, it was not possible to examine any examples of handwriting dating from the period before he met Jane, so any assessments had to be based on what survived from his maturity, and chiefly from the period 1873-1882. Each sample differed in style, but one was of particular interest, for George apologizes to his wife 'for the manner in which this letter is written'. It is the only one written naturally. The writing reveals a personality who had a mental picture of himself built up in youth, from which he never deviated. George saw himself as strong, reliable and friendly, and believed himself possessed of great charm. He wished to present this image to the world, and believed that others must see him in this light. His writing showed that he was a man driven by his desire for stature and professional prestige. In private he had to be the focus of attention and admiration. He was an incurable optimist, but beneath this façade his self-confidence fluctuated alarmingly. He possessed drive and ambition, but lacked a goal and purpose in life. He was clear-minded and objective, passionate, greedy and sometimes deceitful. The constant effort of playing a part tended to make him muddle-headed and compromised his judgement.

None of this was apparent from the content of the surviving documents themselves. Jane's writing, on the other hand, showed that as she matured she acquired an ease of manner and regularity of behaviour which she lacked in youth. Considerably more documents in her handwriting survive, and considerably more was known about her personality from these. Nevertheless, her handwriting suggested that she became dominated by a material and physical possessiveness, amounting in later years to an emotional sickness. This was something which the contents of her letters did not reveal, although the handwriting most certainly did. Comparing the handwriting of George and Jane, one finds some interesting similarities, which suggests that in many respects they were birds of a feather. In their personal standards, interests and depth of feeling, the evidence of their writing suggests that they were compatible. Both appear calculating and money-minded, but in their respective attitudes to personal distance the seeds of friction can be detected.

Their son Simon was a man of exceptional ability, both artistic and practical. He was an inventor and the founder of a successful business. In extreme youth (and letters from his fifth year to his death have survived as well as a mass of notebooks of a technical nature) Simon's writing is remarkable for the drive and vision it reveals. Research into the childhood environment of famous and successful men has shown that one parent frequently possesses a taste for research, experimentation or adventure, and a need for physical or intellectual activity. It has also shown that a possessive and ambitious mother can channel her thwarted wishes into ambition for her son. An unresolved Oedipus complex can, therefore, be the source of energy whereby the son tries to make the mother happy, feeling it to be his mission to succeed where the father has failed.

George had been a photographer, and his father before him a musician. He had absolutely no business sense, and had eventually gone bankrupt. The grandfather, however, had been a man of European stature, though likewise lacking in business acumen. In Simon's childhood writing an unconscious pull towards his mother is very apparent; so is his strong desire to excel. From a very early age he possessed a great capacity for thinking big and long-term planning. The writing suggests an exceptional ability for getting things done and seeing them through to their conclusion. He appears exceptionally thorough, and had a tendency throughout his life to make doubly sure, and to return constantly to correct what he had previously written.

Simon was a man prepared to observe the conventions of his age, where other men of equally great originality might disregard conventionalities. He was less original as a thinker, though better able to see the potential in other people's ideas and to exploit them with great imagination. This element of conventionality is one which permeates his writing throughout his life, suggesting a wish to proceed by orthodox routes rather than to strike out into fields beyond his own sphere. The writing reveals some strange alternations in his character. On the one hand there is aggression, and on the other humanitarianism, a hard streak balanced by something almost amounting to gullibility, but resulting in an impressionable, easily accessible personality.

About 1884, at the age of twenty, certain changes in his writing began to appear, indicating a versatility of the mind within a set framework. Later these variations increase, reflecting, by 1890, a nervous stress and strain. The most striking feature is the appearance of a halo-like loop above the letter 'k'. This detached movement is a characteristic of the writing of his son Bernard and daughter Sarah, and can even be detected in an embryonic form in his own childhood writing as early as 1872, when he was eight. This and other unconscious features detected in Simon's writing and that of his children, can be clearly observed in the writing of his father and grandfather, suggesting that the origin of certain character attributes can be traced genetically from particular sources by a study of handwriting.

CHAPTER THREE
Surnames:
Their Origin and Meaning

Ever since antiquity, one of the chief requirements of society has been the ability to distinguish individuals by their own name. Originally people had only one name, but as society became more complex, this name became peculiar to the person concerned. At the dawn of Roman history, individuals were given one name only, but with the development of Roman society, a system was perfected to distinguish individuals from each other which resulted in their having up to four names. The first of these was the *praenomen*, followed by the *nomen*, then by the *cognomen* and frequently by an *agnomen*. The *praenomen* was a personal name chosen from a fairly limited number, possibly not more than thirty, and was often repeated within the same family. Typical examples are Caius, Publius, Marcus, Lucius, etc.

The *nomen* indicated the clan or *gens*, and was carried by every male and female member of the same *gens*, even by adopted children and by freed men and foreigners who had become Roman citizens as a result of service to a particular *gens*. The *nomen* is the most important part of a Roman individual's name. It links him directly with his clan, and also to both his ancestors and descendants. It is the symbol of the unity and continuity of the clan. For example, the full name of the Roman Emperor Claudius – Claudius Nero Drusus Germanicus – tells us a good deal about his ancestry.

The *cognomen* or surname indicates divisions of the clan into various families, and in general originated from a physical or moral attribute. The *agnomen* was added to indicate a particular situation, quality or relationship of a person who had been adopted.

Roman society, therefore, perfected rules for the distribution and succession of names comparable to our present system, and which were not found anywhere else amongst the peoples of antiquity.

The Greeks, in contrast to the Romans, tended to give people somewhat fantastic names, or names which had an idealistic ring to them. Many Greek names end in -cles (glory or fame) e.g. Pericles (very glorious); Sophocles (famous for wisdom); Callicles (famous for beauty). Other names began with Cle- such as Cleophanes (radiant with glory). Many Greek names incorporate the word 'aristos' (the best) e.g. Aristophanes (radiant with the best, or emanating goodness).

Whereas these names tend to be poetic, noble, fantastic or idealistic, the Romans in rugged contrast favoured much more prosaic names derived from mundane sources; for example Agricola (farmer); Cicero (a man who grows peas – maybe a peanut farmer!); Porcius (pig breeder); Rufus (red); Longus (tall); Crassus (fat); Balbus (stammerer); Claudius (lame); Plautus (flat-footed); Calcus (blind); Scaurius (club-footed); the list is endless and almost as if culled from the orthopaedic unit of a hospital. The ultimate in prosaic names must surely be those derived from numbers, such as Secundus (second); Tertius (third); Quartus (fourth); Quintus (fifth); Sextus (sixth) and so on. These names even became diversified into Quintilianus, Sextius, Octavianus and so on. It is almost as if fathers could not be troubled to find names for their offspring, so just called them two, three, five or whatever.

An element present in Greek names, but only in a minor way, reflects religion and an awareness of God. In the countries of the Middle East, and especially amongst Arabs and Jews, names referring in some way to God are extremely common. Many Jewish names incorporate the syllable Ja, Jo or Je, short for Jehovah or Jahwe, and begin or end with El, both of which mean God. For example Joshua (whose help is God); Jokanaan (John) (whom God has given); Jehosaphat (to whom God has done justice); Obadaiah (in Arabic Abdullah – God's Knight); Elimelech (to whom God is King); Eliezer (to whom God is help); Nathaniel (God-given); and Joel (a double reference to God, i.e. God is Jehovah). Even abbreviated names such as Nathan, which is short either for Nathaniel or Jonathan, contain this God element.

Ancient Teutonic names likewise reflect the characteristics of that warlike race. A strong preoccupation with heroes, war and fighting distinguish the Germans of antiquity. War and a thirst for adventure according to Tacitus (far from silent as his name implies), were what the Germans were best known for, and the 'Furor Teutonicus' is reflected in their names. The words for weapon, war, struggle and victory are at the root of most ancient Teutonic names. *Hild*, *gund*, *had*, *bad* and *wig* are ancient Teutonic words for struggle, battle and war, which have disappeared from the German language as it is spoken today, but which entered Britain with the Angles and Saxons, and which survive today, as for example in Wyman from Wigmund, and Hathaway from Hadawig.

Germans, more than other European peoples, have tended to keep their ancient names. Names such as Otto, Hermann, Heinrich, Adelbert, Dietrich and Bernhardt are all of Teutonic origin. These names spread outwards from Germany and by the time of the Crusades they were found belonging to Frenchmen, Italians and Normans. For example Godfrey (Gottfried) de Bouillon, Robert of Normandy, Raymond of Toulouse, Boemund of Taranto. In 991, many of the French bishops who gathered at the Synod of Reims had German names; e.g. Adalbert of Laon, Godermann of Amiens, Odo of Senlis, Ratbod of Noyon and several others.

After the fall of Rome, it was not until the eleventh century that it was again felt necessary to distinguish individuals by more than one name or to distinguish every clan or stock by a surname. The *cognomen* or family surname which has now been incorporated legally into society originated towards the end of the tenth century. It is true, however, that a few great families were distinguished by surnames as early as the ninth century, but only a very few documents have come down to us from this remote period to show which names were used as surnames transmitted from father to son and which were used as second names or nicknames.

The essential characteristic of a surname is its continuous transmission from father to son indicating the stock from which a family descends. In Italy, the Venetians were the first to use surnames. A document dated 982 signed by Baduarius Bragadino, Vitalis Greco, Johannes Bembo, Dominicus Maurocene and Dominicus Contareno among others, is the earliest surviving example.

There must be tens of thousands of differently spelt British surnames, but their modern form is comparatively recent, often preserving a phonetic spelling found two or three hundred years ago in some parish register or manorial roll.

Some British surnames sound very foreign; indeed a great many are of German, French, Scandinavian and Jewish origin. But the name Pharaoh, for example, has nothing to do with Egypt but is a reconstructed spelling of Faro, originally Farrer, found also as Farrey, Farrah (made famous by the manufacturers of Harrogate toffee) and Farrow. The Sussex name of Van Ness has as little to do with Holland as its variant Venis has to do with Venice. Both are variants of a French place name Venoix in Normandy, where one of William the Conqueror's knights held land before the Conquest. Other variants of this name appear as Veness and Venus – nothing to do with the erotic activity of one of its bearers.

People nowadays are very particular about the correct spelling of their surnames, but a fixed spelling has generally only been adopted since Victorian times, and one cannot therefore assume that a distinctive spelling found in the past and continued to the present indicates continuity of line. The whims of scribes and the dictates of fashion had more influence on the spelling adopted from time to time than any other factor, particularly as most people were illiterate and signed with a mark.

We are fortunate in the English-speaking countries that the custom – though not the law – has long been that the children of a marriage assume the father's surname. Certainly in England this has been the case since medieval times, but in Wales there was a system of patronymics until recent centuries by which there was one name for each generation, linked to the previous one by the appellation 'son of'. The Scottish and the Irish clan/sept systems have resulted in the suppression of Celtic surnames, the acquisition or imposition of substitutes, and the limitation to a clan name.

Thus a surname, better than any pedigree, can take one back in the male line over twenty generations or more and then back again, more indefinitely, as a byname or forename, perhaps, to a person of Saxon or Norman or even Danish origin.

Surnames became fixed and hereditary over a long period and were in common use from about the beginning of the sixteenth century. No laws were made on the subject (and there are still none) and no conscious decision in any one generation to adopt a surname and make it hereditary; it was all very much a matter of convenience, both personal and administrative. Before this time, as again is the custom now, 'Christian'-names sufficed for daily use.

Surnames may be divided into five main groups:

1. Surnames of relationship, that is to say deriving from the father's name (patronymic) or mother's name (matronymic) – Johnson, Alisson.

2. Surnames deriving from offices, titles, professions or trades – Judge, Lord, Parson, Tailor.

3. Surnames deriving from places or country of origin, from feudal fiefs and from topographical features – London, French, Ecclestone, Hill.

4. Surnames deriving from plants, fruits, flowers and animals – Quince, Bull, Tree. This is a particularly popular category among Italians, where an eccentric king of Naples once decided to award his courtiers titles of nobility, all of which were connected with vegetables, hence: Duca della Verdura (Duke of Greens), and Conte Carotti (Count Carrots).

5. Surnames deriving from nicknames – Cruickshanks, Goosey, Sharp, Wise. A sub-division of this category contains what may be termed phrase names, such as Purefoy – pure faith; Godsave or Godsalve. Such nicknames have the crudest of origins. There is the famous story told by John Aubrey in his *Brief Lives* of the courtier who, on making a profound obeisance before Queen Elizabeth I, had the misfortune to break wind. He was so overcome with embarrassment that he went into voluntary exile for many years. On his return home it happened that the Queen met him on one of her Progresses. With a tact not perhaps as great as that of her latter-day namesake Elizabeth II, the Queen said 'Sir, we greet you. We have forgot the fart.' It was no doubt an ancestor who committed the same faux pas at the French Court, who earned for Marshal Pétain the name of Roland Le Péteur.

In the nineteenth century the fashion for multiple surnames began to appear. One of the earliest examples is Ashley-Cooper, dating from the late seventeenth century, but with the union of aristocratic or politically influential houses, the habit increased. When John Churchill, Duke of Marlborough, died without a male heir, his daughter combined her surname with her husband's to produce Spencer-Churchill. They were followed by the Cavendish-Bentincks, Montagu-Douglas-Scotts, Twistleton-Wykeham-Fiennes, Ernle-Erle-Drax and even Cave-Brown-Cave. Generally speaking this custom grew out of the wish to perpetuate the name of a family which would otherwise have died out for want of male heirs. In earlier times the surname was given as a first name, so that one can find in the sixteenth or seventeenth century such names as Bassingbourne Gawdy, Moundeford Kirby, Seckford Gosnold, where the given name is usually that of the mother's family or more rarely the surname of a godparent from whom it was hoped the child would receive a substantial legacy. Nowadays the tendency is to drop one of the two surnames, as for example, the family of Lord Brabourne, the late Earl Mountbatten's son-in-law, who now call themselves Knatchbull, whereas they were formerly Knatchbull-Hugessen.

Some surnames that have disappeared in this country are still alive and well and flourishing in America and Australasia, while others have assumed different forms in those countries, particularly the United States, for a variety of reasons. Taken down by 'foreign' clerks, uttered by descendants unfamiliar with the place from which they originally hailed, if a locative name, they became distorted in the process and then formalized in this condition when spellings became fixed during the last century. Conversely, in many cases foreign names have accidentally or purposely become disguised as English names, so that now they cannot be told apart, with sometimes traditions or legends accruing to support their supposed origin, so that we are back again to the parallel of the modern Englishman who accepts unchecked family stories as to the origin of his own name and family. However, in general, the surnames of modern America reflect ethnic origins and though the United States and Canada are chiefly English-speaking, the names of their inhabitants reflect the polyglot nature of Europe.

CHAPTER FOUR
Where to Begin:
Family Sources and Traditions

The first rule for the family historian is this: always work from the known to the unknown. This is the principle adopted by all police forces the world over, because it is the one which produces results which stand up to the most critical examination in courts of law. This may, perhaps, seem a somewhat stark approach to family history, but if you wish to create a pedigree that truly records your ancestry and which is worth handing down to posterity, then it is essential.

Probably most of us have family legends of lost fortunes and vast acres that should by right belong to us. Many have been told of an ancestress who was 'taken advantage of' by the Duke of Blankshire, or that we really belong to the landed gentry, or have blue blood in our veins. Grandmother, for example, may be convinced that her husband, long since dead, was a descendant of, shall we say, the Percys. On investigation, however, it may turn out that he was only the son of a man who lived in Alnwick. It is indeed possible that the descent is genuine, as in the case of Frederick Howkins mentioned by Sir Iain in the Foreword; on the other hand everything could be thoroughly above board and the only connection may turn out to be that of employer and employee.

A very large number of Americans are convinced that their ancestors came over the Channel with William the Conqueror, and over the Atlantic in the *Mayflower*. This is fascinating romantic stuff, but the genuine family historian should be seeking fact not fiction. Since a surprising number of people can genuinely trace their ancestry to King Edward III, as Sir Iain pointed out in the Foreword, the legend may not be so fanciful after all, but the point is it must be proved. Many traditions become exaggerated or diluted to become 'more acceptable', particularly the latter, for our Victorian ancestors were adept at locking skeletons in cupboards and sweeping dirt under carpets. It is therefore not advisable to accept everything at face value, yet traditions nevertheless carry a grain of truth, and should be borne in mind as they may help to point out a line of research which otherwise would be overlooked.

It is not always possible to establish a connection with a distinguished family of the same surname. This is a trap into which the descendants of many emigrants tend to fall. Howard, for example, is an extremely common surname, sometimes deriving from Hayward – an official found on every manor in the land – and sometimes from the old German for high or chief warden, and occasionally from the old French Huard which in turn derives from the old German, literally translated as brave heart. But because the premier English peer, the Duke of Norfolk, happens to have the surname Howard, people tend to jump to the conclusion that they are his kin. The chances of being related to such families is remote indeed. For names like Churchill, Townsend, Russell or Spencer derived in the first two instances from place names, Russell comes from red or 'russet', and Spencer from dispenser (of provisions), i.e. Steward or Butler. Indeed, what about Stuart and Boteler? If you are related to one of the prominent families bearing these names, the fact will automatically emerge in the course of research, and will be all the more rewarding for being accurate and substantiated by archival evidence.

Fortunately it is unnecessary to start research from such abstract points, for by applying the principle of working from the known to the unknown, the search is taken backwards generation by generation to the most remote ancestor the records can reveal. Having decided which particular surname is to be researched, initial enquiries will be directed towards one particular family. However, if you are undecided which line you wish to trace, it will be necessary to obtain as much information as possible from all branches of your family group. In this way it is possible to chart your genetic descent from both parents, four grandparents, eight great-grandparents and sixteen great-great-grandparents – always supposing you have that many. It is one of the ironies of genealogy that those with the bluest blood have the fewest ancestors, for the tendency among the aristocratic and dynastic families for cousins to marry each other reduces at a stroke the number of grandparents from four to two.

Those who attempt to trace their genetic ancestry frequently encounter the problem of a Jones, Smith or Brown ancestor, which effectively can block their path. At this point it is as well to pass on to a less common family surname, and undertake detailed research into that line instead. In practice, however, most family historians tend to keep to one surname only.

The most valuable and rewarding information will come from your eldest relatives, and it is logical to start by consulting them. If your surname is comparatively uncommon, it is often worth writing to people of the same name whose addresses you can find in the telephone directories. Some of these may well turn out to be remote cousins and they may have oral or documentary evidence to help in the building of a pedigree. As for family traditions, oral evidence is not always completely accurate, so allowance must be made for incorrect names, dates and places, which may have to be amended later when reliable documentary evidence is found.

An interesting example of this kind of problem relates to the American family of Langhorne. Family tradition, handed down over several generations, suggested that the family originated in the Welsh village of Laugharne and from a family of that name which owned large estates in Pembrokeshire in the seventeenth century. It is easy to see how this mistaken tradition arose, if one is unaware of the fact that the Welsh name is pronounced monosyllabically 'Larne'. The American family pronounces its name 'Langen' and the confusion arose from the mis-transcription of several documents in the printed Calendars of State Papers where a Colonel Richard Laugharne sometimes appears as Colonel Richard Langhorne. Anyone can be forgiven for confusing the written letters 'u' and 'n', and 'a' and 'o'. These were in fact two quite distinct families and it was not very difficult to disentangle the confusion once it was realized how the initial mistake had arisen.

Family Bibles are a most valuable source of evidence, for the records of births, christenings, marriages and deaths were usually made at or near the time of the event, and are therefore usually reliable. It is important, however, to check when the Bible was printed, for it is by no means unknown for the original Bible to disintegrate with wear and to be replaced by a new one, and for the entries either to be incorrectly transcribed or even entered from memory.

Copies of birth, marriage and death certificates may be found among family documents. Associated with these certificates may be baptismal certificates, wedding invitations and memorial cards, and because these are printed close to the time of the event, they are usually accurate records. The same applies to Confirmation and First Communion certificates, Barmitzvah cards, marriage contracts and settlements, and divorce settlements.

Records of academic and professional attainments are useful sources of information, particularly service records such as discharge papers. School prizes and certificates, university degrees, sporting prizes and cups, certificates of ordination, club and association records, trade union cards, apprenticeship indentures, trade and guild records, freedoms of cities, testimonials, civic awards, medals and decorations – all these add flesh to the bare bones of a pedigree and give clues to age and hence date of birth. In addition to these basic facts, they indicate abilities, interests and achievements in a way no other sources do. They can also point to the direction from whence some of your own interests and characteristics derive.

Records relating to property are valuable for the light they throw on the movements of a family from one place to another. Maps, passports, identity cards, denizations, naturalizations and letters, both personal and official, provide much information about a family, for they record major events in the lives of the individuals and families concerned.

Another type of record relates to wealth and health. These include bank books, stocks and share certificates, annuity (tontine) certificates, medical certificates, driving and other licences.

Finally, there are personal documents and mementos which may include pedigrees or notes on aspects of the family's history, which if not authenticated by a body such as the College of Arms, will need checking for accuracy. In this category fall diaries, personal letters and scrapbooks which, if subjected to handwriting analysis (see Chapter 2) can add greatly to one's knowledge of the character of the writers. Birthday books and cards, account books, book plates, samplers, which frequently include the age of the person who worked them and where and when they were made, armorial silver, china and glass, mourning and signet rings, seals and fobs, and of course portraits and photographs of people and houses are all very valuable. As an example of the way in which a picture of a house can help, a Canadian had a picture of a Georgian house in Somerset in his family album. It was taken about one hundred years ago, and the caption underneath it included the name of the house and the words 'God Bless our Home'. There was no one in the family who knew why it was in the album, nor the name or the relationship of the person who put it there. A letter to the present owner elicited a number of interesting facts, including copies of the deeds from which it was possible to discover that the house had been let for twenty years between 1860 and 1880 to a family which, on investigation, proved to have been that of one of his great-grandparents, whose name he did not even know. From this it was ultimately possible to discover when this particular individual had been born, married and emigrated, and why.

Naturally, a number of these items could be in the possession of distant members of the family, possibly those who descend from female lines and whose surnames are different from your own. Care should be taken when approaching such people not to give the impression that as the family historian of your particular branch, you are the person to whom they should belong. Whenever possible, offer to have the material copied at your own expense, or make arrangements to photograph it yourself. Since much research of this kind must be carried on by correspondence, often with elderly people who may be easily bothered by receiving letters asking numerous questions, and who may not be in the habit themselves of writing long letters, the response may be negative. Wherever possible it is a good idea to seek a meeting, and to record your conversation on tape. An excellent example of this technique is to be found in Ronald Blythe's marvellous book on Suffolk village life *Akenfield*, which is almost entirely based on tape-recorded interviews. When approaching people for family information, it is advisable to take or send a separate pedigree of the family group, and ask for comments, corrections and additions where appropriate. Ask if there are any documents available for copying, and if your correspondent knows of any other members of the family who might have information to offer. Always enclose a stamped addressed envelope or two International Reply Coupons.

If you do not know of any direct contacts, but know the town or county from which your ancestor came, then an enquiry through the personal column in the appropriate local newspaper or county 'countryside' magazine could bring results. Head the advertisement with the surname you are researching in bold type. Most people stop to read anything about their own name, or one that is well known to them. Follow this with a brief explanation of the research project, asking anyone with information or similar interest to contact you at the address shown. If the surname is a common one locally, much of the information may be irrelevant, on the other hand it may put you in touch with distant kinsfolk who are unknown to members of your family.

CHAPTER FIVE
Printed Sources

After getting all the information you can from family sources, and before embarking on extensive research in manuscript archives, it is wise to find out whether any work has been done before on the families in which you are interested, or whether anyone else is currently engaged in research with whom you might exchange information.

Two valuable books available at most principal libraries are G. W. Marshall's *The Genealogist's Guide*, and J. B. Whitmore's *A Genealogical Guide* which is a continuation of Marshall's work. These books form a valuable index to pedigrees of three generations in the male line that have appeared in print before 1953. T. R. Thomson's *A Catalogue of British Family Histories* and G. B. Barrow's *Genealogist's Guide* are more recent works containing additional information which complement Marshall and Whitmore. Margaret Stuart's *Scottish Family History*, Joan P. S. Ferguson's *Scottish Family Histories held in Scottish Libraries* and Edward MacLysaght's *Irish Families, Supplement to Irish Families* and *The Surnames of Ireland* are the appropriate works for those countries.

When you first set out to discover what printed books about your family there may be, time can be saved by a visit to the British Library, but admission to the Library is by pass which is available only if you are over twenty-one years of age. Provided you take proof of identity, such as a passport, banker's card or similar document bearing your signature, a pass can be obtained without much difficulty, once you have been photographed in the Research Admission Office. However, if you wish to have access to the Department of Manuscripts, you will need a written reference from someone of recognized position, such as a clergyman, lawyer, or schoolmaster, certifying that you are fit to use the Students' Room of this department. Because the demands on staff have increased so dramatically in recent years long delays in the production of books and documents must be expected.

In order to find out what printed sources on the particular family you are interested in there are, you must consult the main catalogue where printed family histories are listed under the relevant surname. These may include privately printed volumes of memoirs and diaries as well as family histories themselves.

Under the Copyright Act, the British Library is one of six libraries to which a copy of every book published in Great Britain since 1814 must be sent. The other Copyright Libraries are the Bodleian, Oxford, the Cambridge University Library, The National Libraries of Wales and of Scotland, and Trinity College Library, Dublin. You will thus find a number of extremely useful standard works, including *Walford's County Families, Victoria County Histories*, sundry county and parish histories, genealogical periodicals, the *Gentleman's Magazine* – a goldmine of information in the form of obituaries and articles of family interest, *The Dictionary of National Biography, Who Was Who*, and many more. The Manuscript Department is particularly valuable for collections of family papers, diaries, genealogies and the huge collection known as the Harleian Manuscripts which contain copies of many of the pedigrees taken at heraldic visitations extended by subsequent historians.

It is worth mentioning that once you have listed the books which interest you in the main catalogue, most can be obtained through the inter-library loan scheme from your local public library.

Many County Libraries and County Record Offices have collections of local family genealogies which are easy to locate as they are almost invariably indexed.

Many pedigrees, not all of them armigerous, are registered at the College of Arms in London, or at the Lord Lyon Court in Edinburgh, the two official bodies with jurisdiction over the granting of arms in England and Scotland. The corresponding body in Ireland is the Office of the Chief Herald of Ireland at Dublin Castle. The College of Arms does not allow public access for research, but searches can be undertaken by officers of the College on the payment of a fee. In Edinburgh and Dublin the registers are open to the public. Nevertheless, there are several standard reference books on heraldry such as, for example, Fox-Davies' *Armorial Families*, Debrett's and Burke's *Peerages*. Burke's *Family Index* is a general guide to family entries featured in their range of genealogical and heraldic publications since 1826 and is of great value to family historians.

In addition to these generally available sources, there is a large collection of family histories and pedigrees at the Society of Genealogists in London, which houses the largest specialized library on the subject in Britain. Non-members can make searches in the Society's Library for a daily fee.

The National Genealogical Directory, which is available through most local libraries, lists the names and addresses of many hundreds of family historians, and many thousands of surnames of families currently being researched. Similar directories of 'members interests' are published by local family history societies, which are now established in every English county and parts of Wales, Scotland and Ireland. Now nearly every county has such a society, and the address of your local society, or the one in the county from which your family may have originated, can be obtained from The Federation of Family History Societies in Birmingham. For those who decide to embark on a definitive study of a particular surname, it is advisable to contact The Guild of One-Name Studies which is the co-ordinating body for the growing number of family historians who concentrate their research on references to a single surname only.

CHAPTER SIX
Manuscript Sources

Civil Registration

No matter how much information has been obtained from family and printed sources, the exciting time will come when you have to embark on original research of your own. For the family historian the progression of research is in the main logical so long as the axiom of working from the known to the unknown is adhered to. Inevitably the first public records required to extend a family history are those of civil registration of births, marriages and deaths.

The starting date for civil registration was not uniform throughout the United Kingdom. In England and Wales it started on 1 July 1837, and the country was divided into Registration Districts under the control of a Superintendent Registrar whose records contain all the original certificates for the events that were registered within that district. At the end of each quarter – March, June, September and December – a copy of all registered events is sent to the Registrar General at St Catherine's House in London. These are collated into master indexes for births, marriages and deaths for the respective quarters, but it must be emphasized that the entries in them relate to when the event was registered, and not to the date it actually took place. If therefore you are looking for an event that happened near the end of a quarter, it may not be registered until the beginning of the next one.

Anyone can go to St Catherine's House to examine the indexes of births and marriages or to nearby Alexandra House to examine the indexes of deaths. Such searches can be carried out free of charge. It should be borne in mind, however, that these places become very overcrowded, particularly during school half-terms and holidays as well as between 12 and 2 pm. Therefore these times should be avoided as much as possible.

The distinctive bindings of the indexes – red for births, green for marriages and black for deaths – make it easy to locate the section required. Within each volume, all entries are arranged in strict alphabetical order. Because surnames are liable to variant spellings, however, it is advisable to make a list of all these so that each can be checked if the entry required cannot be located where you expect to find it. For example, a family named Langman might be indexed under Longman. The name Kirby can be spelt more than thirty ways phonetically. Because the letter 'b' in seventeenth-century script can be mistaken for 's' and 's' can be mistaken for 'f' the name could appear (and, indeed, has) as Kersie and Kerfitt, for 'tt' can be mistaken for a final 'e'.

You should start by looking at the volume where you think you will find the entry of your known family member. When you have found the volume you require for the appropriate quarter and year, and the particular name of the person you are looking for, it will then be necessary to note the various references shown against that name. The full entry indicates the surname, forename(s), registration district and the volume and page number on which the actual entry is recorded. This information, together with the year and quarter, are required for completing the application form to obtain a copy of the full certificate. You will need the full certificate as the short one is of little value for genealogical purposes, since it omits details of parentage and gives the date and place of birth only.

There are certain 'peculiarities' for each main section of the indexes which are worth noting. The indexes from the September 1837 quarter to the December 1865 quarter are handwritten on vellum and are split into a number of alphabetical volumes (a note of caution: these can be very heavy to handle). The details given are as previously described. Unless there are more than three, each forename is written out in full. In the year 1866 the indexes are printed, and for this year only the second and any other forenames are only shown by initials. From 1867 to 1911 these indexes are printed with most of the forenames.

In 1911 we witness the beginning of typescript indexes with again only the first forename being shown. From 1912 onwards, the surname of the mother is recorded in the birth indexes, immediately following the surname and fore-name(s) of the child. This can be a valuable check that the entry is the correct one, provided, of course, that the mother's surname is known. This is also helpful in compiling a family group from the index entries without the expense of obtaining certificates for all the children born to a particular family. Some mothers' surnames are the same as the surname of the child. Although this can be a case of marriage between cousins, it quite frequently signifies a birth out of wedlock. In the Marriage Indexes the surname of the other party is also shown after 1912. This again is a check that the entries are correct, if both surnames are already known. With marriages, both parties are indexed under their respective surnames; therefore it is always essential to check both the entries (assuming both surnames are known), in order to obtain the certificate, the district, volume and page number for both parties must be identical. Here sometimes one has to search a number of years if your particular ancestor was the youngest of a large family. Do not despair if you do not find a marriage quickly. The Death Indexes show the age at death, after the forename(s) from 1866 to 1968. After 1969, the date of birth of the deceased is shown instead of the age at death, which may or may not be accurate.

The information shown in each full birth certificate is as follows:

1. When and where born;
2. Name, if any;
3. Sex;
4. Name and surname of father;
5. Name, surname and maiden surname of mother;
6. Occupation of father;
7. Signature, description and residence of informant;
8. When registered;
9. Signature of registrar;
10. Name entered after registration.

If at the time of registration the forename(s) of the child have not been decided, the 'Name, if any' column will be left blank, and the entry in the index will show the surname, followed by either 'male' or 'female'. However, if the forename(s) were ultimately notified to the registrar, then they would be recorded in the last column, headed 'Name entered after registration'.

If the child was born out of wedlock, in most cases the name of the father is not shown, and the child is registered under the surname of the mother. However, since 1875 the father's name may be inserted, in which case the birth is registered under both surnames.

If the mother had previously been married, then the column 'Name, surname and maiden surname of mother' would show, for example, Jane Brown, late Smith, formerly Jones. But if the informant did not reveal this information, it will not be shown, and could therefore read Jane Brown, formerly Jones.

If you cannot find the entry of the person required in the main index, but other members of the family group are known, it is worth looking for one of these entries, and if you find it, obtaining the certificate as this will provide you with the information regarding the parents. This procedure is recommended because of the surname variants previously mentioned, which, apart from phonetic misinterpretation, can be caused by incorrect copying from the original registration.

Full marriage certificates contain the following information:

1. When married;
2. Name and surname of both parties;
3. Ages;
4. Condition (bachelor, spinster, widow, etc.);
5. Rank or profession;
6. The residence of both parties at the time of marriage;
7. Fathers' name and surname;
8. Occupation of fathers.

If the names of both parties are known, then it will be easier to locate the relevant index entry for the less common surname first, and then cross-check this with the other party's index entry for the matching references previously mentioned. If the bride is a widow her surname will be that of her late husband; but if a divorcee then it may be her previous married surname or her maiden name. Sometimes a woman has been living with her husband before the marriage, and may have changed her name to his by Deed Poll. Consequently she will be listed in the index under her changed, but lawful surname, and if declared at the time of registration, also under her original surname.

If the name of one or the other or both fathers is missing on the full certificate, this may be due to several reasons: the party was born out of wedlock, the father was deceased, or at the time of registration the information was not recorded. The last two instances are cases of negligence, but such cases are known to have happened. Some marriage certificates will show the name of the father together with the word 'deceased'. There is, therefore, no point in looking for his death registration after the day on which the marriage took place. On the other hand, the fact that 'deceased' is not recorded on the certificate is not proof that the father was in fact alive, as at the time of registration this particular question may not have been asked.

The ages shown on marriage certificates can be misleading. They may have been increased or decreased at the whim of the parties involved. Unfortunately, many are recorded as 'of full age', meaning that the people were twenty-one years old or upwards. Often '21 years' can indicate the same thing, merely that the person was of full age. The 'Residence at the time of marriage' may not always be the usual place of abode of the bride and bridegroom, but may be a temporary address of convenience. It is well worth noting the religion and occupation shown on marriage certificates, since these may be important clues to other records, and to the identification of people elsewhere.

Death certificates contain the following information:

1. When and where died;
2. Name and surname;
3. Sex;
4. Age;
5. Occupation;
6. Cause of death;
7. Signature, description, and residence of the informant;
8. When registered;
9. Signature of registrar.

It should be remembered that the place of death may not be the usual residence of the person who has died. In fact you may find that the deceased died many miles away from home. This can be helpful if he was visiting relations at the time, since it could guide you to an area from which the family originally migrated.

The age given can be incorrect and allowance must be made for this when calculating the probable year of birth. It is of course very helpful if the informant is a relative as the relationship may be stated which can confirm a tentative link in your research.

All certificates show places of residence, and if the events occurred near the date of a census, they offer a useful clue for searches in the Returns immediately following or preceding them. Although the records of births, marriages and deaths registered in England and Wales since 1 July 1837 are the main class of records held by the Registrar General, there are others which are worth noting. Records of still-births registered in England and Wales since 1 July 1927 can be obtained only with the special permission of the Registrar General. Records of births and deaths at sea (known as the Marine Register Books) since 1 July 1837 relate to persons born on British ships whose parents were born in England and Wales. Records of births and deaths in aircraft began in 1949 (known as Air Register Books) and relate to these events occurring in any part of the world in any aircraft registered in Great Britain and Northern Ireland. Service records contain births, marriages and deaths among members of the armed forces and certain other persons, or occurring on board certain ships and aircraft. Royal Air Force Returns began in 1920. The registers of the Army are in two series. Firstly, there are the straightforward registers of army records and chaplains' returns, and secondly there are the indexes of Regimental birth registers. Equally there are the equivalent registers of marriages and deaths which are not indexed but can be sought on personal application in the foreign department of St Catherine's House. There are also separate death registers of officers and men who died in the Boer War and Second World War for each of the services.

Entries of births, marriages and deaths for civilians which took place in foreign countries can be found in either the Consular Records which are kept at St Catherine's House or the Miscellaneous Records which are held at the Public Record Office. These comprise what is known as the Overseas Section which is probably the most apt term for describing a group of registers made up from various sources.

The Consular registers were started in 1849 by an Act of Parliament and continue until the present day. Miscellaneous registers are non-statutory ones which were sent into the Registrar General. They have now been sent to the Public Record Office and both the indexes and the registers can be seen at Chancery Lane unless they are less than thirty years old. The earliest of these are registers of births, marriages and deaths that took place at The Hague from 1627. There are also some eighteenth- and nineteenth-century records which begin before 1849. If you fail to trace your particular family in the Consular registers, then you should consult the Miscellaneous register.

Records for anyone born in one of the former or existing British Colonies are held by the Registrar General of that country except for those records held by the India Record Office for British citizens born in India before 1947.

The last registers to be mentioned here are of British persons, civil or military, in the Ionian Islands from 1818–1864 who were in either Cephallonia or Corfu.

Records of adoption consist of entries made in the Adopted Children Register, in accordance with the Adoption Acts, since 1 January 1927, and relate only to adoptions effected under these Acts.

In recent years the fee for full certificates has changed so frequently that it is advisable to ascertain the current charges from the Registrar General at the time of undertaking your research. Applications by post will be undertaken but the cost is currently more than double that of going to the General Register Office in person. Fees for searches are given in the free leaflet available from the Registrar General.

Divorce records in England and Wales date back to 1852. However, it is necessary to know full particulars of names and the approximate dates of the Decrees Nisi and Absolute. Applications for the Decree Absolute should be made in person or by post to the Divorce Registry in London.

Apart from the obvious information obtainable from certificates, there are a few points worth noting which could also be of use. A note should be kept of all witnesses and informants that are shown on certificates as they could be relatives or provide links with other evidence for future research. It is possible that a few events were not registered, especially births, and the possibility is greater before 1875 because from that date the penalties for non-registration were increased. If, even after trying all possible surname variants, the search in the general indexes fails to produce results, then the period of search should be extended progressively either side of the expected date of the event. If the district where the event took place is known, it is advisable to try the district Superintendent Registrar's Office, in case of errors or omissions in the general indexes. Lastly, it may be that the event took place abroad, in which case either occupation or family connections may provide a clue for further research.

The Channel Islands and The Isle of Man

In the Channel Islands civil registration is divided between Jersey and Guernsey, each having their respective Registrars General. In Jersey births, marriages and deaths have been recorded since August 1842, and information about them can be obtained from the Superintendent Registrar, in Jersey, but research enquiries should be addressed to the Société Jersiaise, St Helier.

The States of Guernsey has jurisdiction over the islands of Guernsey, Alderney, Brecqhou, Herm, Jethou and Sark. Registration of births and deaths is now governed by an Order-in-Council of March 1935 and registration of marriages by an Order-in-Council of May 1919. For the period before this, but after 1840, completed registers are held by the Registrar General in St Peter Port, Guernsey. It should be noted that some of the registers of Alderney were lost during the German occupation in 1940–45.

In the Isle of Man the statutory records of births and deaths relate to those registered since 1878 and marriages since 1884. In addition there is the Adopted Children Register which covers legal adoptions registered since 1928. Search fees are very reasonable and enquiries should be made to the General Registry, Douglas, Isle of Man.

Census Returns

The Census Returns have been described by some researchers as the most helpful and revealing records that the family historian is likely to encounter. As early as 1750 it was proposed that regular censuses of the population should be held, but it was not until 1801 that they were introduced. Since that date they have been held every ten years with the exception of 1941. Unfortunately the returns up to and including 1831 are generally of little use from the family historian's point of view as the names of residents were not recorded. It is therefore those from 1841 onwards that are of interest. In England and Wales the census returns are not available for public inspection until they are over one hundred years old.

The original returns are held at the Public Record Office in London, on micro-film, but before access to them is allowed it will be necessary to obtain a Reader's Ticket from the Enquiry Office or a day pass at the door.

It is at this stage in your research that the addresses revealed by previous work can be of such value. The nearer the date on the records which reveal such addresses is to the date of each census, the greater the possibility that the person being sought will be found at that address when the census was taken.

The census of 7 June 1841 records the parish or township, and the name of the city, borough, town or village at the head of each enumeration sheet. The columns beneath show:

1. The name of the street, place or road and the name or number of the house;
2. The name and surname of each person in the house;
3. Age and sex;
4. Rank, profession or occupation;
5. Whether born in the same county;
6. Whether born in Scotland, Ireland or foreign parts.

The ages and persons under fifteen years are stated exactly, but those above fifteen years are rounded down five years, i.e. someone aged sixty-four appears as sixty, twenty-three as twenty, and so forth. Places of birth are indicated by 'Y' (Yes) or 'N' (No) and 'S' (Scotland), 'I' (Ireland), 'F' (Foreign parts) in the appropriate columns.

The Returns of 1851, 1861, 1871, 1881 and 1891are far more informative. They show the following additional information:

1. The schedule number;
2. Relationship to the head of the family;
3. Condition or matrimonial status;
4. The exact age of each person;
5. The exact parish and county of birth;
6. Whether deaf, dumb or blind.

In the 1871 census, provision was made to show if any person was an imbecile, idiot or lunatic. All the above applies to the 1901 and 1911 Census Returns when they become available. The dates on which the censuses were taken are important: 30 March 1851, 7 April 1861, 2 April 1871, 3 April 1881, 5 April 1891.

It must be noted that those listed in the Census Returns are every person living in the house on the day in question, together with those engaged at their labour during the night, and returning regularly next morning. No member of a household who normally slept away from the house was included, such as domestic staff, residents at an institution, and so on. Such persons would be recorded on the appropriate enumerator's return, at such places as hotels, lodging houses, hospitals, institutions, aboard ships, and even in tents. Visitors and servants are often listed in the household and their places of birth are worth noting as there may be some form of family connection in that area. Occupations are frequently abbreviated, e.g. Ag. Lab for agricultural labourer; F.S. for female servant; Ind. for independent means; and so on.

The marks made by the enumerators after a list of names for a given address are to indicate, / the end of a household, and // the end of all households within the building. On some returns, particularly those for small villages, the name of the street or road is not shown, and the only identification given is that of the schedule number. To ascertain the likely location of the house or building concerned it will be necessary to check the 'description of enumeration district', which is to be found at the beginning of each such section of the census return. In any case, you can save many hours of searching by checking the description of each district first, to see if the street or road is listed as part of that particular enumeration. If it is not found, then each subsequent district should be checked until the place required is located. Roads of great length are invariably part of more than one district, in which case all districts may have to be checked before the required address is found. Sometimes an address cannot be found, owing to a change of house name or number, or even the name of the road itself, between the date on the source of information and the date of the census. In such cases, the Record Office should be consulted in order to find out whether a list of such changes exists for that particular locality.

For large towns and cities, street indexes are available, and these are of considerable help in locating the section of the census return required to find a particular address.

It is also worth searching the area in the vicinity of the family residence. In the past, members of the same professions and family groups often lived near to each other, and the returns, by noting the trades or professions of those living in a locality, shed a great deal of light upon its social make-up. It must be stressed that the information recorded in the Census Returns is subject to varying degrees of error. False statements were made by those who had something to hide, or were just being awkward. Ages can be found to be only approximate; there is also the perpetual problem of surname variants due to spelling or phonetic misinterpretation.

Nicknames, stage names and noms-de-plume are sometimes found in Census Returns. In one case the individual's given name was Ernest but he was always known in the family as George because he liked this name better. Unless one has information of a private character it is usually impossible to identify such people with certainty, and much confusion is caused thereby. Bella for Isabella, Nelly for Helen and similar variants are very common and frequently found in returns.

In addition to the Public Record Office, most County Record Offices and many reference libraries have copies of the Census Returns for their areas. Although the Census Returns are only available for public inspection if over one hundred years old, it is possible to obtain information for more recent returns from the General Register Office, London. However, in these cases it is necessary to provide the surname and christian name of the person, and the precise address, together with written permission of that person or a direct descendant, and to sign a declaration that the information will not be used in litigation. The fee required for this is quite high, and consequently this is a source only to be used as a last resort.

Census Returns in the Channel Islands and Isle of Man are held in the public Record Office in London.

Parish Registers

At this stage of research, the accumulated evidence from certificates and Census Returns will provide the names of your ancestors and the approximate dates of events and places where they were living in the early nineteenth century or late eighteenth century. It is at this stage that the records of the Parish and its administration will provide the main sources for these and earlier generations.

Of the many parish records available for research, undoubtedly the Parish Registers are the most important. The earliest registers in England and Wales began in 1538 when Thomas Cromwell, Vicar General to Henry VIII, issued an injunction that records of baptisms, marriages and burials should be kept by the clergy of the Church of England. These early registers are generally paper books, and few originals have survived. It is estimated that from more than 11,000 ancient parishes less than seven hundred have registers that go back to 1538. The remainder have registers that begin at various dates between then and 1597, and some even later than that. It was in 1597 that, for their safer keeping, parchment registers were ordered to be kept and that the earlier entries in the paper registers should be copied into them. Unfortunately the wording of the Act which referred to the copying of the earlier registers included the phrase 'but especially since the first year of Her Majesty's reign' (1558). This provided a loophole for the lazy who were looking for an excuse to limit copying to forty rather than sixty years. The Act also provided for transcripts to be made from the registers within a month after Easter for the previous year for submission to the bishop's registrar. These transcripts are generally known as Bishop's Transcripts and are usually deposited in the Diocesan Record Office. The original Parish Registers come in a great variety of shapes and sizes, but of more interest is the way in which they were written up. Most of the details of an event would be made in a notebook or on slips of paper by the incumbent or parish clerk and according to the size of the parish, entered into the register later at various intervals, when they remembered. It does not, therefore, need much imagination to see that as a result of this custom, some events were either lost, written up from memory, or entered in the register out of chronological sequence. This, together with the fact that some registers were divided into three sections – baptisms, marriages, burials – others in chronological order with the events mixed according to the sequence in which they happened, and yet others used three separate registers, means that very thorough and careful checks must be made during research, unless the registers have been completely transcribed and indexed.

During the Commonwealth (1648–1660) many clergymen were forced to leave their parishes, especially if they were Royalists. Some took their registers with them, some buried them for safety with the result that many were lost or irreparably damaged, and other registers were destroyed when Cromwellian soldiers plundered the churches. From September 1653 until the Restoration, Parish Registers (i.e. registrars) were appointed to record births, marriages and deaths with the Justice of the Peace to perform civil marriages. In some parishes the registers were well maintained, some to an even better standard than under the old system. In the majority of parishes, however, the standard deteriorated drastically and there are many instances where no records were kept at all during the whole period.

Due to the serious decline of the English wool trade, an Act was passed in 1678 that all the dead were to be buried in wool with a fine being imposed for non-compliance and an affidavit was made by a relative or associate of the deceased. Consequently 'Affid' or 'Affdt' can often be seen after a burial entry in the register. The Act was repealed in 1814, but had ceased to be enforced long before that date.

In 1694 'for carrying on the war against France' a duty was levied on a sliding scale for non-paupers of 2s. for a baptism or birth, 2s. 6d. for a marriage, and 4s. for a burial, rising to the considerable sum of £30 for the baptism of a Duke's eldest son, and £50 for a Duke's marriage or burial. The duty was abolished a few years later as it proved to be unenforceable.

During the eighteenth century both the Church and the State were concerned about the increasing laxity in performing marriages by clergymen who had been conducting ceremonies with scant regard to the status of both brides and grooms. This state of affairs was resolved in 1754 by Lord Hardwicke's Marriage Act which introduced separate marriage registers on printed forms which required the entries to be signed by the officiating minister, the bride and groom and two witnesses. The Act also reinforced the requirement that all marriages must be preceded by the calling of banns, for three successive weeks, unless a licence was granted, and marriages were only to be solemnized in a Parish Church.

The only exceptions to this rule were marriages of Quakers and Jews, since their records were considered satisfactory, and they were therefore allowed to continue conducting their own marriage ceremonies.

Hardwicke's Marriage Act did not eliminate clandestine marriages. Determined couples made for Gretna Green and other places across the Scottish border and for the Channel Islands, where the regulations were less stringent than in England.

Marriage licences and banns are a subject of importance. The great majority of British marriages were by banns (or 'proclamation'). The couple's intention to marry was announced on three Sundays in their parish churches – or between 1653 and 1660, it could be proclaimed in the nearest market-place on three market-days – to allow anyone knowing of any 'just impediment' to declare it.

Licences, however, were issued by the Church authorities, and these enabled people to marry immediately without banns. Apart from the obvious human need for a hasty marriage those who used them were the prosperous, who wanted to avoid publicity; soldiers and sailors who might be called away at short notice and had no home parish anyway where banns could be called; anyone whose freedom to marry needed to be clarified or (before about 1700) who wanted to marry at the religious seasons of prohibition (Lent, Advent, etc.).

The records (if they exist) of a marriage licence were the 'allegation', a declaration on oath by the bride and bridegroom of their freedom to marry; the 'bond', a record of security given by, usually, a close friend or relation of the truth of this; the 'licence', a document authorizing marriage, often at a stipulated church; finally there was often a register kept of the licences issued.

Licences were normally issued by bishops and archdeacons, or their officials, and the records are among the other archives of those dignitaries. However, where the parties to be married lived in different bishoprics, then strictly the licence should have been issued by the archbishop, although this rule was often broken.

The Stamp Act of 1783 imposed a duty of 3d. on all entries in Parish Registers, which was extended two years later to cover Nonconformists. As paupers were exempt, an increasing number of ordinary citizens declared themselves as such in order to avoid the duty. Once more, many poor people failed to have their children baptised. As before, this second attempt to raise revenues through the Parish Registers failed, and the Act was repealed in 1794.

The final piece of legislation of importance regarding Parish Registers is Sir George Rose's Act of 1812 which provided printed form registers for baptisms, marriages and burials that remained the standard form of registration until the introduction of Civil Registration in England and Wales in 1837. As the three principal Church ceremonies continue to the present day, it is of course possible to extend research in the Parish Registers beyond 1837. In fact, as previously stated, during the early years of Civil Registration by no means everyone obeyed the law, and it may be that recourse to the registers will solve an otherwise insuperable problem.

As a result of the Parochial Registers and Records Measure of 1978 a large number of original parish registers have now been deposited in County Record Offices and Diocesan Record Offices where many are being transcribed and indexed. In 1974 Local Population Studies, in association with the Cambridge Group for the History of Population and Social Structure, published the first of its handbooks entitled *Original Parish Registers*. This, together with its supplements, is a list of original parish registers which have been deposited in Record Offices, Libraries and other institutions in England and Wales. The list is arranged alphabetically by county, and alphabetically by parish within each county. It includes original parish registers, rough books of register entries, duplicate books made simultaneously with the registers, and early replacement copies such as those ordained in 1598. It excludes original parish registers still in the possession of incumbents, later copies and all non-Anglican registers. Another useful guide to parish registers is Frank Smith's *A Genealogical Gazetteer of England*, an alphabetical dictionary of places with their location, ecclesiastical jurisdiction, population and date of the earliest entry in the register of every ancient parish. The Gazetteer, be it noted, does not include Wales, Scotland or Ireland.

In the Isle of Man, the earliest records of the Church of England date from 1611 for baptisms, 1629 for marriages and 1610 for burials. All enquiries to the General Registry,

Douglas. Information about Channel Island Registers can be obtained from the addresses given in Appendix V.

Religious toleration in England was unknown before the Declaration of Indulgence in 1672 under which Protestant dissenters secured licences for the conduct of worship according to their own consciences in their own meeting houses. They had met together for many years, of course, and a few had kept registers, but these were of baptisms apart from the Society of Friends (Quakers), who had no ceremony of baptism and recorded birth instead. Following Lord Hardwicke's Act of 1753, valid marriages could only be performed by the clergy of the Church of England and by Quakers and Jews, and this remained the law until the introduction of Civil Registration in 1837. Even then, Nonconformist ministers were not allowed to perform burial rites in parish churchyards until 1880.

A Royal Commission was appointed in 1836 to enquire into the state, custody and authenticity of the 'non-parochial' registers, and to recommend means for their collection and arrangement, legal use and availability. The registers were collected following the Non-Parochial Registers Act of 1836, mainly from most but not all Baptists, Congregationalists, Presbyterians, Methodists, and eventually from the Quakers and some other denominations. The Jews and the majority of Roman Catholics refused to part with their registers which remained in their own custody. The registers were transferred to the Public Record Office in 1961 and comprised 7,000 volumes and files. Before the Quakers surrendered their registers, indexed digests were made. One copy was deposited with the local Quarterly Meeting, and another at the Library of the Society of Friends in London. Also included in this category of records at the Public Record Office are unauthenticated registers of baptisms and marriages performed at the Fleet and Kings Bench Prison, at May Fair and at the Mint at Southwark, which had been deposited in the Bishop of London's Registry in 1821. With one exception – the register of the Independent Church at St Petersburg in Russia – the deposited registers relate solely to England and Wales, but include several registers of Huguenot and other foreign Protestant churches.

In addition there are the headquarters, libraries and museums of various Nonconformist communities which contain extensive records for research. The Baptist Union Library; United Reformed Church Historical Society, which covers Congregational and Presbyterian records; Independent Congregational Library; Huguenot Library; Methodist Archives and Research Centre; and Unitarian Church Headquarters. Enquiries relating to Roman Catholic records should be made to the Archbishop's House in London, or at the local diocesan archives. Jewish records are housed at the Jewish Museum in London and at local synagogues.

Entries relating to Nonconformists often occur in Anglican parish registers; marriages occur as an inevitable consequence of the legislation already mentioned; burials often occur as a practical necessity as many Nonconformists had no burial ground of their own; baptisms are particularly found for the various Methodist divisions, as they originally saw themselves as members of the Church of England, and not dissenters. Also, for some years after 1696, Anglican clergymen were obliged to record births of Nonconformists.

In recent times various classes of Nonconformist records have come to light and have been deposited at the appropriate County Record Office, where it is always advisable to make enquiries.

In many parish churches, monumental inscriptions and tombstones supplement information derived from the registers. Consideration should be given to the parish churchyards, Nonconformist burial grounds and cemeteries authorized by the Act of 1853, which also allowed many cities and boroughs not only to open public cemeteries but also enabled the church and chapel yards to be closed when they were full. There were also private cemeteries which had opened prior to the Act and many more since. Some inscriptions have been transcribed and copies are deposited at the Society of Genealogists, the appropriate County Record Office or library, or the British Library. There is also considerable work being undertaken by local societies to record as much as possible before natural wear and tear, churchyard clearance schemes and vandalism destroy them forever. Registers of local cemeteries are usually kept by the local government authority. If you are able to locate an ancestor's memorial the inscription, including the verse, can contain clues to occupation and career and should be recorded in full and when practicable, photographed. It is also advisable to look for related burials in the surrounding area as many families wish to be buried close to each other. If it is hard to find out where a burial took place, a search in the British Library, Newspaper Library or the County Library in local newspapers for obituary notices may help.

Possibly the greatest contribution made by the Church of Jesus Christ of Latter Day Saints is the recording of parish register entries by births (baptisms) and marriages on computer files. The International Genealogical Index, as it is called, consists of many millions of entries from the parish records of many countries. These are available for examination on microfiches and are of the greatest value in establishing the distribution of surnames at any particular period from the sixteenth to nineteenth centuries. A word of warning must, however, be given about the use of the IGI. Much of the information fed into the computer comes from printed or manuscript transcripts of the original registers, and while every effort is made to see that all the entries are accurate, mistakes do occur. For example, when investigating the Bickley family recently it was discovered that many names were listed under the name Buckley. These entries were taken from the parish of St Leonard, Shoreditch, which when the original registers were examined showed clearly how the mistakes had arisen. Furthermore, since only identified infant burials are included in the IGI it may turn out that the individual for whom one is searching and whose name one discovers at about the right time and in the right parish in fact died. This would not show up in the IGI, and one could be led badly astray if one were to rely solely on it. Also some areas are less well covered than others.

Other Parochial Records

Until comparatively recently many social services now undertaken by the State or the Local Authority were the responsibility of the parishes. It is consequently necessary to take account of how the parish was administered, and the type of records this produced.

The administration of the parish was vested in the clergymen and church wardens, of which there were usually two. Primarily their duties were to ensure that the fabric of the church was maintained, and to administer the property and money for which they were responsible. The records they left are usually called the Vestry Minutes and Churchwardens' Accounts, both of which can contain evidence of value to the family historian as they mention persons to whom payments were made, or from whom money was received for the upkeep of the buildings, purchases of commodities, payment of rates, and other business that will establish informative facts about particular parishioners. In addition, they provide historical material that is of exclusive interest to that particular parish in question.

However, the records of major importance for genealogical research are those of the overseers of the poor. In the sixteenth century, the problem of the poor was acute and vagrancy was widespread due to the dissolution of the monasteries and the increase of enclosures.

By legislation culminating in the Great Poor Law Act of 1601 normally two substantial householders were nominated each year to be Overseers of the Poor, with the duty of maintaining the poor and setting them to work, the funds being provided by parish rates. Further acts required that Houses of Correction should be built for 'rogues, vagrants, lewd women who have bastards, and parents leaving their children chargeable to the parish who shall be brought before the Justices for committal'.

Later legislation established the law of settlement and removal which contained the provision that any strangers settling in a parish might be removed by the Justices unless they rented a tenement of not less than £10 annual value or found security to discharge the parish of their adoption from all expenses that may be incurred upon their behalf, or they brought a 'settlement certificate' from their own parish accepting liability for any charges. The act also authorized the justices to transport to the plantations in the colonies incorrigible rogues, vagabonds and sturdy beggars. Further legislation provided that serving a parish office, paying a parish rate, residing in the parish, being bound apprentice by indenture to a parishioner, or, if unmarried, serving a year in the service of the parish established settlement.

There was also concern about the prevention of vagrancy, and in 1743/4 a reward of 5s. was introduced for the apprehension of any vagrant and removal, after whipping or confinement, to their place of settlement. Incorrigible rogues were treated more harshly. After six months' imprisonment, with whipping at the Justices' discretion, they were either sent home or impressed into naval or military service. Persons sheltering vagabonds were fined a sum of from 10s. to 40s. Vagrants' children could be apprenticed by the justices, and bastard children of vagrant women were not to gain a settlement in the parish of their birth. They were in fact hastened from one parish to another to make sure that the baby was born under someone else's haystack. This treatment caused a scandal, as a high proportion of mothers and babies died as a result of this policy.

Throughout the eighteenth century there was considerable litigation between parishes. A parish would claim that someone was settled elsewhere; the individual concerned would then be examined before a justice, reciting his life history in a document of fascinating detail; his legal place of settlement would be determined and he would be sent there; if the receiving parish had doubts about the legal settlement, a re-examination would be ordered. All efforts were concentrated on avoiding one's own parish having to pay relief. The consequent proceedings, of course, are of great genealogical value.

In 1781/2, because of the 'incapacity, negligence or misconduct' of Overseers, and the 'sufferings and distresses of the poor being most grievous', provisions were made for the inspection of workhouses, and no poor were to be sent into a workhouse more than 10 miles from their own parish, also no persons except the indigent were to be sent to the workhouse, and no children under the age of seven years were to be forcibly separated from their parents.

A further act in 1792 dealt with the abuses of the removal of vagrants. In future, no reward was to be paid for their apprehension until they had been punished, and no female vagrant was to be whipped for any reason whatsoever. In 1794/5 no person was to be removed until they were actually chargeable, and the justices were authorized to suspend at their discretion orders of removal upon sick and infirm people. It was also in 1795 that the meeting of Berkshire justices at the George and Pelican Inn at Speenhamland took place. This gave its name to the ill-advised Speenhamland System under which a scale of relief, based on the size of the family and the price of bread was devised. It never received statutory recognition, but the example was followed throughout the country, and tables showing the 'Speenhamland Act of Parliament' were displayed in ale houses for the edification of their clientele.

Following a Royal Commission of Inquiry, which reported scathingly on the whole system of parochial poor relief, the Poor Law Reform Act of 1834 was passed. Under this act, the responsibility was transferred from individual parishes to groups of them in Poor Law Unions. The major events in the subsequent history of the Poor Law were the transfer of its administration from the unions to the county councils in 1929, and, finally, the assumption by the central government in 1948 and 1966 of responsibility, not only for the broad lines of 'public assistance' and 'social security', but also for much the greater part of its detailed administration.

It may come as a surprise to learn that in the sixteenth century the birth of illegitimate children seems to have been an unusual event. Such an occurrence was becoming more common in the seventeenth century, and so common as to create little surprise from about 1750 onwards.

The concern shown in this matter by the parish was not solely a moral one, as there was also the more material problem of maintenance on the parish rates. Therefore, if the father could be identified, he was made responsible for the maintenance of the child. If, therefore, the parish register only gives the mother's name, a record of the father's may be found elsewhere among parochial records.

Most poor children were bound apprentices at an early age. By the eighteenth century the old rules governing apprenticeships were disappearing, and they were often used as a convenient way of providing for a pauper child. Most were indentured to learn husbandry or housewifery in their own parish, and this usually resulted in them being used as agricultural labourers or female servants. Those apprenticed elsewhere were indentured to a variety of trades, rarely skilled ones. However, there were abuses of pauper apprenticeship. For the worst, one must consult the records of the mills in manufacturing towns and villages which imported pauper children by the wagon-load from London, contracting to take 'one idiot in every twenty', where the conditions were indescribably horrible, and where the graveyards hold scores of the small bodies of these unfortunates who were literally worked to death.

The Parish Constable was chosen annually from the residents of the parish, and men usually served in rotation. The Constable was appointed by the Justices of the Peace of the county, and was responsible for maintaining law and order, caring for the stocks and whipping post; the apprehension of rogues, vagabonds and others, and bringing them before the magistrates; the arrest of those ordered to appear in court; administering punishments to convicted offenders; accompanying vagrants and others to the House of Correction; and various other relevant duties as required. By 1856 the office of Parish Constable had been superseded by the county and town Police Force or Constabulary. The records of the constables throw much light on the activities of parishioners.

Overseers of the Highways, or Waywardens, looked after the roads and bridges in the parish. They had to pay for the upkeep of roads, which resulted in taxes being levied in the parish. The accounts of the Overseers, where they survive, show who owned property and paid taxes, and also show payments to contractors and individuals who did the work required, and are therefore useful as background material.

The Parish Clerk kept the minutes of the Vestry Meetings, cared for the parish registers and Banns Book, and sometimes led the singing in church. Other duties may have included being the sexton (gravedigger) and caretaker of the church and churchyard. The Sexton's Book, if available, gives details of burials, and often contains far more information than the burial entries in the parish register.

Each county and borough had its Court of Quarter Sessions, and it not only dealt with criminal cases, but also performed the duties of local government before county councils existed. Typical of such matters are those ensuring that the major highways were kept in good repair; paying coroners for their inquisitions; committing vagrants and others to the House of Correction; committal and release of debtors from gaol; payment for burial of those who died whilst passing through the county; inspection of workhouses and, if warranted, bringing the parish officers to court for orders to be made against them; bodysnatching cases; poaching; and instructions and orders to the parish constables.

Finally there are the Charity records. Charities of early

medieval foundation still exist, and in early times they were almost invariably entrusted for administration to the parish clergymen and churchwardens. Some typical charities concerned themselves with food, education, loans, clothing, skilled apprenticeships for poor children, and coal and fuel.

In all the parish records we have mentioned it is almost certain that somewhere you will find a mention of your ancestors, no matter what their status within the community. Apart from providing valuable evidence of their existence, these records give a fascinating insight into the type of persons they were, and create a picture of the environment in which they lived.

The great majority of these records are now deposited at County Record Offices and it is always there that you should first enquire.

The Problem of Dates Before 1752

The generally known basic fact, and for many purposes all that need be considered, is that before 1752 the official English calendar reckoned the year as beginning on 25 March ('old style' or O.S.) and from 1752 the year was reckoned from 1 January ('new style' or N.S.), and that it is customary to show the year by double indication for dates between 1 January and 24 March; thus for example 24 March 1715 should be written 24 March 1715/16, and the following day would be 25 March 1716. The double indication can be found in some registers before 1752.

This much is quite well known, but there were complications which affect church registers. The fact that both were changed in one year by the New Style Calendar Act has obscured the point that there were two quite separate factors involved: (a) the 25 March new year was English practice from the twelfth century until 1751; (b) England used until 1752 the Julian calendar which incorporated a miscalculation of leap years; this had been amended by Pope Gregory XIII to produce the Gregorian calendar in 1582; this was promptly adopted in Catholic countries, but, as a 'popish invention', less readily so by Protestant countries. Most of Europe had been using the 1 January new year before 1582. The New Style Calendar Act made two changes in the official calendar: (a) with effect from 1 January 1752, the calendar year was reckoned from 1 January and (b) eleven days 3–13 September

1752 were omitted to adjust to the Gregorian calendar, with adjusted calculation of leap years thereafter.

The English colonies including North America used the official English calendar; Scotland, however, adopted a 1 January New Year in 1600, although retaining the Julian calendar; Britain and its colonies were, therefore, ten days (1582–1700) or eleven days (1700–1752) out of phase with the calendar used in much of western Europe.

In the first place, and although surprisingly the fact seems to have failed to be noticed in any standard reference sources, it seems to have been quite widespread practice for a 1 January calendar year to have been used in earlier sixteenth century registers. A few examples survive, but it seems that many registers were altered to a 25 March year when they were transcribed onto parchment in about 1600; the registers of Chudleigh, Devon, and Fareham, Hampshire, show that the transcribers got into a muddle when changing the dates. Some modern transcribers of registers have also adjusted the dating of their work to a 1 January year basis, rather than preserving the text of the original document, which can cause confusion.

The earlier Presbyterians also had a tendency to use a 1 January new year basis before 1752; for example Tavistock Abbey Chapel registers record in 1693 'N.B. the year is supposed to begin from that we commonly call New Year's Day' and date the records accordingly. This may be in part attributable to a significant number of ministers with Scottish names, presumably used to the Scottish calendar. Similar tendencies can be found among denominations with continental European links; Catholics, Huguenots and Moravians in particular. (One register of a Moravian congregation in London goes so far as to date entries before 1752 by both the Julian and Gregorian calendars.)

The Society of Friends used official English reckoning for the year but objected to months and days of the week named after heathen gods. They used a numerical system, Sunday being 'first-day' and Saturday 'seventh-day'; months before 1752 were March, 'first month' round to February, 'twelfth month'; thus the calendar year started on the 25th of the first month. (The months September to December, being Latin numeration concurring with Friends' numeration, were acceptable.) From 1752, this was changed, January being 'first month' and December 'twelfth month', and this was specified by a printed notice circulated in September 1751 to all meetings in Great Britain, Ireland and America, from the London Meeting for Sufferings.

The Jewish calendar is an extremely complicated subject, outside the scope of this book beyond stating that the Jewish epoch dates (by Christian reckoning) from 1 October 3761 BC, and the year varies between 353 and 385 days in twelve or thirteen months. A detailed account can be found in the *Encyclopaedia Judaica*.

CHAPTER SEVEN
Wills, Administrations and Inventories

Wills and their associated documents are a particularly important record for the family historian. Often they are the only truly personal document a person has left, and the only clue we have to them as people rather than names on a piece of paper or parchment. But, as you will see, they are a complicated subject.

Much of the text of a will is of less relevance to genealogists and so the text can often be summarized. It was customary, for example, to start the will with the set-piece declaration of faith; for example,

In the name of God, Amen. The sixth day of December in the year of our Lord God one thousand six hundred fifty and fower I, William Currer of Middleton in the parish of Ilkley and county of Yorke, yeoman sick of body but of perfect memory (praysed be God for it) doe ordaine and make this my last will and testament in manner and forme following: First I commend my soule into the hands of Almighty God my Creator who gave it trustinge by the onlie merritts and mediacion of his sonne and blessed Saviour Jesus Christ . . . And my body to the earthe to be buried in the parish church of Ilkley aforesayd at the stall-head where I had my seat formerly at the discretion of my friends And for my worldly goods that God hath beene pleased to bestow upon mee my will and mynde is that they shalbe to 'such and such' uses' as hereafter shalbe expressed.

The whole of this lengthy preamble and committal can be summarized as follows: 'William Currer of Middleton, Ilkley, Yorks, yeoman. Will made 6 December 1654. To be buried in the parish church of Ilkley. Usual committal.' The will continues as follows:

Item I give unto Dorothy my wife the third part as the law doth require of all the remainder of my goods.

Item I give unto my sonne Henry Currer twenty pounds as
a legacie to be paid within one year next after my decease
to be put forth for his use.
Item I give unto my five children Henry Currer my sayd
sonne Alice Currer, Jane Currer, Mary Currer and Anne
Currer my daughters.

and so on in greater or less complexity, and often including
long complicated legal provisions governing the descent of
property and the management of the estates of children who
were under age. This particular will ends thus:

Item I make Dorothy Currer my sayd wife and Henry my
aforesayd sonne sole executors of this my last will and
testament Sealed with my seale and signed the day and
yeare above written: William Currer. Sealed and signed in
the sight and presence of us Thomas Ferrand Agnes
Ferrand Thomas Guyland.

At the end of the will there will be the probate act, in this
case in English because the will was made during the
Commonwealth, when, from 1653 to 1660 all wills were
proved centrally in London. Usually the probate is in Latin,
but the form is very much the same, except that the name of
the ecclesiastical court is given.

This will was proved at London the sixth day of February in
the year of our Lord God according to the computation of
the Church of England one thousand six hundred fifty and
five before the Judges for probate of wills and granting
administrations lawfully authorized by the oathes of Dorothy Currer the relict and Henry Currer the naturall and
lawfull sonne of the sayd deceased joynt executors named
in this last will and testament of the deceased to whom was
committed administration of all and singular the goods
chattels and debts of the sayd deceased they beinge first
sworne by vertue of a Commission well and truly to
administer the same.

The researcher can abbreviate the will and probate as
follows:

will proved 6th February 1655/6 at London by exors. Wife
Dorothy Currer and son, Henry Currer. Witnesses: Thomas Ferrand, Agnes Ferrand, Thomas Guyland. Supervi-

sors – none. Bequests to the Poor – none. Legatees: Wife, Dorothy Currer one third of estate. Son, Henry Currer, £20 to be paid within one year of death. To daughters Alice, Jane, Mary and Anne Currer (all under 21) remainder of goods equally divided. Wife, Dorothy to have education of son, Henry (under 21) and youngest daughter, Anne. Each child to be the others' heir. Property. Tenantright of farm at Middleton, Ilkley and land called Hard Inges. Profits of whole to Dorothy till son reaches 21, thereafter Dorothy to have half for life, but if she remarry, she to have Hard Inges only for life. If son dies before 21 daughters to inherit.

Since January 1858 wills in England and Wales have been proved centrally at the Principal Probate Registry at Somerset House in London, and in Ireland at the Principal Probate Registries in Dublin, and, since 1922, Belfast. The law governing wills in Scotland is different from that in the rest of Britain; testamentary matters in the Channel Islands and in the Isle of Man are still in the jurisdiction of the local courts. Annual indexes of Grants of Probate and Letters of Administration in England and Wales can be consulted at Somerset House free of charge. Copies of wills and administrations may be consulted for a fee.

Before the establishment of the Principal Probate Registry the probate of any will in England and Wales took place in one of at least three hundred courts depending upon the location of the estate of the deceased. There was a hierarchy of church courts; at the head were the Archbishops' Prerogative Courts of Canterbury and York (PCC and PCY) and the local courts of the Bishops and Archdeacons. There were also areas of 'Peculiar or exempt jurisdiction of Church and other dignitaries' which did not come under the Bishops or Archdeacons' Courts at all.

Probate records of the land-owning classes and the wealthy are most likely to be found in PCC, at the Public Record Office – for which there are printed indexes to 1700 and a consolidated card index 1750–1800 at the Society of Genealogists (in course of publication). The Prerogative Court of York, of which the records are at the Borthwick Institution at York, filled the same role for the northern province (Cheshire, Cumberland, Durham, Lancashire, Northumberland, Nottinghamshire, Westmorland and Yorkshire). Their records were not solely confined to the wealthy, and the indexes and calendars should always be searched in addition to those of local courts.

Details of the exact jurisdiction of each court, the location of their records, and the existence of printed and other indexes, are given in two books: *Wills and their Whereabouts*, by Anthony J. Camp (1974), gives full details of all types of probate records in each diocesan and other record office, and describes the probate procedure fully; *Wills and Where to Find Them*, by J. S. W. Gibson, (1974) is more clearly presented, arranged by (historic) county, with maps to show jurisdictions, and is designed specifically for the inexperienced; either will set the searcher for probate records on the right path. These two books also give details of probate records in Scotland, Ireland, and in the Channel Islands and for the Isle of Man (for which probate matters are still dealt with locally). Many testators elsewhere in the British Isles also had property in England and Wales, so their wills also may appear in PCC. Another book which the researcher will find useful is *A Simplified Guide to Probate Jurisdictions* by J. S. W. Gibson published by the Federation of Family History Societies and Gulliver Press.

Properly speaking, a 'will' deals with real estate, though under Scottish law before 1868 and certain Channel Islands law only personal (i.e. movable) property could be bequeathed. A 'testament' deals with the bequest of personal goods such as clothing, furniture, stock, farming implements, trade tools, bonds, book debts or money in any form; hence the phrase 'last will and testament'. In cases of intestacy or where there was a defect in the will the next of kin or a creditor applied for letters of administration. The Administration Act was entered in a book and there was also the Administration Bond whereby the administrator gave security for acting properly. It was usual to submit an inventory of the deceased's goods with the will, and almost invariably with administrations especially before about 1720. Inventories are sometimes found filed with wills and sometimes separately, as in the case of wills and administrations proved in the Prerogative Court of Canterbury, and as they list the deceased's possessions, are a fascinating record for a family historian.

Estate Duty Registers

Legacy or death duty was first introduced in 1796 and was a tax payable on legacies and residues of personal estate of deceased persons. The estate duty registers and their indexes are available for inspection in the Public Record Office in London for England and Wales. The registers begin in 1796 and continue until 1894, but can only be read if they are 125 years old. The indexes, however, can be consulted for the whole period. Before 1812 there are separate indexes for each court, later a single consolidated index.

Estate duty registers can be a valuable aid to the family historian in finding in which court a will was proved or an administration granted. They contain a good deal of useful information which may supplement the will itself. For example, in the will you may find that the testator has stated 'to all my children' or other such persons unnamed as such. In these registers the names of the legatees and their relationship to the deceased are given. These registers also show the name of the deceased, the date of the will, the place and date of probate, the name, address and occupation of the executors, details of the estates, legacies, annuities and the duty paid.

To find out whether an estate was the subject of litigation, references should be made to the Register Books (Calendars) PROB 12. In *some* of these volumes *some* of the causes are indicated by an entry 'By Sent' (By Sentence) or 'By Decree' as a marginal note by the name of the deceased. Only in the Acts of Court Books (PROB 19) the loose Acts (PROB 33) is there a mention of every case which came before the court. From 1660 to 1782 (PROB 3, 4, 5, 13 and 16), 1782 to 1852 (PROB 31) and before 1660 (PROB 2) records of inventories can be found. These PROB numbers should be checked as they are subject to amendment and additions.

The Irish Public Record Office in Dublin has consolidated indexes of wills and administrations from all Irish courts from October 1829 to 1879 and abstracts from 1829 to 1839, originating in the Inland Revenue Office.

Information from closed registers may be given to the direct descendants or heirs of the deceased on application to the Capital Taxes Office, Minford House, Rockley Road, London W14 0DF.

CHAPTER EIGHT
Land Records

Although the number of people who own their own house is greater today than it has ever been, the fact remains that the records attached to land ownership and tenancies generally provide a valuable source of genealogical information.

Records of this cover a large range of sources spanning a thousand years or more of history. Probably the best known of all is the Domesday Book, a survey of his kingdom ordered by William the Conqueror in 1086. The Norman system of land tenure was based upon military service, and to ensure an effective army land was granted in return for knight-service defined in terms of quotas of armed men, The inventory of his kingdom was made so that the King could know not only the number of towns, villages and manors he and his barons possessed, but also their revenue and population. It was carried through with a degree of thoroughness unequalled until modern times, and the feudal system it established endured for several centuries. However, within each estate (called a 'manor') tenancies continued in a way which had begun before the Normans arrived.

Essentially there were two types of manorial tenant, those who were free and those who were villeins or 'bondmen'. In his turn the Lord of the Manor held his land from a higher noble who held his land from the King in return for military service. Free tenants gave military service or paid rent, villeins had the use of the land in return for work on the lord's land. In time both the Crown and the lords of the manor found it more convenient to commute both the military and farming services for money and to hire men to do the work required to run their estates or to fight their battles. The villeins' land was held according to the custom of the manor and its transfer from one tenant to another, frequently on the death of a tenant when it would usually pass to his son, was recorded in the Court Rolls of the manor. The tenant's evidence of title was by a copy of this, thus the term 'copyhold' tenure. But the Manor Court did not confine itself to matters to do with the transfers of tenancies only. Such officers as the reeves, tithingmen and haywards were appointed annually by the Manor Courts, which also dealt with the enforcement of the customs of the manor, the punishment of petty misdemeanours, and the settlement of minor disputes between tenants and neighbours. It is obvious, therefore, that if you can identify the manor your ancestors were living on, and if the manorial records have survived, you could discover a wealth of valuable information.

Coming nearer to our own day, title deeds, Land Tax Assessments, mortgages, Hearth Tax Returns, Window Tax returns, Enclosure Awards, tontines and annuities, insurance and tithe records all yield a vast amount of information about all manner of people in all walks of life, and not only the so-called landed gentry.

Similarly connections between families and between different generations of a single family can be deduced from a study of title deeds enrolled on the Close Rolls, which extend back to the twelfth century. These generally concern grants of land and privileges by the Crown to individuals and corporations including monasteries, chantries and charities. In 1599, for example, Peter Page bought land from William Kirkeby of East Hatfield, Yorkshire, yeoman, which had formerly been part of the lands of the Yorkshire Priory of Nunkeeling. Deeds in the Close Rolls showed that this land had formerly belonged to Roger Kirkeby and that it had descended to his son Christopher who had died without issue, and that then it came to William, Christopher's younger brother, then to William's son Roger in 1582.

In the Close Rolls for 1630 a deed is recorded between Martin Button of Bath and Capt. Robert Kirby of Woodbridge in Suffolk on one part and Sir William Withipoll and his son, Francis, on the other. Among the lands included in this transaction, which mainly concerned the estate of Sir William Read of Osterley Park, in Middlesex, were some which formed part of the lands of Nunkeeling Priory.

The common factor between these two transactions was of course Nunkeeling Priory, for there was otherwise nothing to connect Capt. Robert Kirby of Suffolk with William Kirkeby of Yorkshire. However, on closer investigation it was discovered that the Nunkeeling Priory estate was bought at the dissolution of the monasteries by Sir Richard Gresham and

John Thynne of Bath. Sir Richard Gresham's great-niece was Lady Rebecca Seckford, whose granddaughter was the wife of Robert Kirby of Woodbridge. Robert Kirby's great-grandfather, Andrew Kirby, according to heraldic evidence, came from a family settled since the tenth century in Lancashire, whose branches extended into Yorkshire.

Land records, therefore, can be invaluable in providing information about families from which much additional information can be deduced. They can also tell us much about the day-to-day lives of our ancestors, and especially about fluctuations in their fortunes. Most of these records were written in Latin up to 1732, which can be a problem for the amateur researcher. Many Manorial Rolls are in County Record offices (not always in the obvious county), in the Public Record Office, in the British Museum and in private hands. A list of known manorial records and their whereabouts can be seen at the National Register of Archives.

While it is possible to use title deeds as genealogical sources without knowing much or anything about the law of real property, it is, all the same, advisable to have a passing acquaintance with the law. It must be realized, for example, that fines and recoveries represent fictitious transactions aimed at circumventing certain statutory prohibitions on the transfer of title. Similarly, a conveyance by lease and release was devised for a specific purpose. A useful brief introduction to the significance of title deeds is Pamphlet no. H 72, published in 1968 by the Historical Association of Great Britain, entitled *Title Deeds 13th–19th Centuries*, by A. A. Dibben.

Basically, a conveyance of land is between two parties, a party in this context being one or more individuals. A deed may be a simple conveyance of a freehold interest in land from A to B or a lease for a term of years from C to D, or be increasingly complex in conveying extensive estates, creating trusts, remainders and entails for generations to come. The more complex thc conveyance the greater the chances of finding genealogical information, for earlier deeds and transactions will be recited and set out, and relationships may be traceable backward for several generations. A series of deeds, both simple and complex, dealing with the same property over a number of years can give a very great deal of information about a family if the property remained in its hands throughout the period. Since it was not uncommon in Britain for families to own property for two or more centuries, the accumulation of deeds and conveyances over this period, even for quite minor families, can be extremely large.

The series of documents known as Feet of Fines not only cover an unbroken period of more than six centuries, but have no parallel in the records of any other country except perhaps some archives in Edinburgh. Beginning at the end of the twelfth century, they continue into the nineteenth. These were records of fictional law-suits over possession of land to obtain the judgement of the Court as to ownership, which was a 'watertight' title. Fines were written in triplicate on parchment. The 'foot', which is the official copy of the document, was retained in the court records and still survives. A typical example, in translation, might read as follows:

This is the final agreement made in the Court of our Lord the King at Westminster in the quindene of Easter in the 7th year of the reign of King Henry VII before A.B, C.D, E.F, Justices of our Lord the King and others there present, etc. between W.X the demandant and Y.Z the deforciant of 8 acres of land and 2 acres of meadow with their appurtenances in Waxham concerning which an assize of mort d'auncestor was summoned between them in the aforesaid Court. Namely that the said Y.Z granted to the said W.X and his heirs all the aforesaid land. To hold to him and his heirs paying therefore yearly 6d. for all service. And the said W.X for this grant gives the said Y.Z three shillings.

Similar records useful in medieval genealogy are the Curia Regis Rolls, De Banco Rolls, and Docket Books of the Exchequer. Another extremely valuable type of enquiry was that which was conducted after the death of many landowners, known as an Inquisition Post Mortem (IPM). On the death of such a man, an enquiry was held to determine the extent and location of his land, and the terms under which he held it. This usually elicits the date of the tenant's death and the name, age and relationship of the next heir. Unfortunately these enquiries ceased in 1645 and were not renewed at the Restoration.

During the English Civil War, landowners who supported the King against the victorious Commonwealth had their lands confiscated by order of committees appointed to investigate the actions of the owners. Having 'confessed their delinquency' and given a pledge to adhere to the Commonwealth, they had to give a full account of their possessions and were then allowed to 'compound' by surrendering a portion of their estate, which varied according to their 'guilt'. The records of these committees (PRO Class SP/23) give a lot of information about the condition of such individuals, often mentioning their heirs and other members of their family. They are known as Composition Papers.

Exchequer Class E 179, at the Public Record Office, London, are records of tax assessments. Among these, the 'Lay Subsidies' are useful because they give the names of taxpayers at the level of wealth taxed that year. They are listed by years and 'hundred' divisions of counties. Also in this class of document are the Hearth Tax returns of Charles II's reign, many of which have been published by local historical societies, and other lists of taxpayers such as some Poll Tax returns. The lists include not only those who paid the tax, but also those who were exempted from paying on account of poverty. This is the only comprehensive list of householders in the late seventeenth century. Unfortunately not all assessments have survived, but these returns are a primary source well worth consulting.

A particularly useful adjunct to subsidy records is in the class E 115 at the Public Record Office; these are certificates of residence for subsidy, and their main value is in effect as a record of 'change of address' where a taxpayer moves away.

CHAPTER NINE

Records of the Services and Professions

Naval Records

Seamen's lives are often depicted as adventurous, daring and exciting. However, underneath the glamour there was another side. There were people who chose the Navy as their career voluntarily, but there were many more who were literally pressed into the 'King's Navy' for what would seem to us a pittance. Conditions were harsh. This was particularly true for those who were below deck. For those above, life was not absolutely cosy either.

The abundance of records that exist shed a great deal of light on these men's lives. Some records give such personal details as what they looked like and even what they ate! This chapter gives a brief summary of those records of particular genealogical interest which are available.

For men serving before the Restoration (1660) no systematic records survive but mentions of individuals on ships are to be found in printed *Calendars of State Papers, Domestic*.

Commissioned Officers

Histories of sea officers' careers can be found in printed books as well as manuscript sources. Taking printed sources one must mention Charnock's *Biographia Navalis* (1794–98), Marshall's *Royal Naval Biography* (1823–30) and O'Byrne's *A Naval Biographical Dictionary* (1849) describing all officers serving in the Navy in 1834. There is also the *Commissioned Sea Officers of the Royal Navy (1660–1815)* published by the National Maritime Museum which presents the dates when officers joined certain ranks. The first manuscript record to look for is the Lieutenant's passing certificate which, depending where you find it, gives you a copy of his baptismal certificate and summarizes his previous training and career.

If you are unlucky enough not to find your man here try and find his Record of Service which will give the dates when he served on a particular ship. From this you can look up the ships' Muster Rolls when he was serving as a Midshipman or as an Able Seaman to seek his place of birth.

Warrant Officers

This term means that they were seamen but were under receipt of warrants. Up to some point in the nineteenth century the commissioned officers were not men who actually navigated ships; this was left to those who were known as the Masters and their Mates. Formally they were only classed as Warrant Officers together with pursers, gunners, engineers, carpenters and boatswains, more commonly known as bosuns. There should be some record for all of these although not all have survived.

Ratings

Before the mid-nineteenth century, generally speaking, it is necessary to know in what ship a man was serving at a particular time. You then use the Muster Rolls which will give details as previously described as well as the ship in which he last served and the date he was discharged from that ship.

From 1853 'Continuous Service Engagement' was introduced. Seamen were given numbers and thus a record of services followed which gives the date and place of birth as well as a physical description and a list of the ships in which he served. For the really ardent researcher there is no end to the length to which he can pursue his studies, like looking up the ships' logs and learning of every single event that occurred in this particular ship. Some of the details may be repetitive like the exact geographical situation of the ship at a particular time of day and the climate, but these logs also record such happenings as 'Seaman Bloggs was insubordinate to an officer, received a hundred lashes on the deck and was sent below'.

These records of services continue up to 1891 and are compiled from when seamen actually joined the Navy. For any records of service of seamen who joined after that date, direct descendants can write to the Naval and Army Records Centre.

Naval Records for Genealogists by N. A. M. Rodger (Public Record Office 1984) is a useful additional guide. Information about naval personnel who served after 1891 can be obtained from the Naval Personnel Records, Room 2007,

OS9(a), Ministry of Defence, Empress State Buildings, London SW6 1TR, and in some cases from the National Maritime Museum, Greenwich SE10 9NF.

The Marines

By an Order-in-Council in 1664 what is now known as the Royal Marines was founded. They were men who not only sailed in ships but also fought on land and therefore were responsible to both the Navy and the Army. Officers' records are in the Admiralty Series. For other ranks you can find your man according to which division he was stationed in; these were at Chatham, Woolwich, Portsmouth and Plymouth. You begin by searching the Description Books and from these you can go on to look for a record of service.

After 1901 records concerning men and officers who served in the Marines are kept in the Royal Marine Drafting and Record Office, HMS Centurion, Grange Road, Portsmouth PO13 9XA.

Coastguards

Basically Coastguards were men drafted from the Navy beginning about 1816. Here all you need know to begin your research is which station a man was serving at a particular time. From there you can trace all kinds of records from his last ship in the Royal Navy to his date of discharge. Coastguards were administered by the Navy but paid for by the Customs. Therefore, a word of warning: sometimes a man will be described on marriage certificates as a Customs officer when he in fact was a Coastguard.

Military Records

Before the Civil Wars (1642–49) there was no regular standing army in England. Regiments were raised to meet a particular requirement and were known by the name of the Colonels who formed them. No systematic records of such regiments survive though references to individual officers and soldiers can be found in State Papers Domestic, Foreign, and other records at the Public Record Office and the manuscript department of the British Library.

After the Restoration (1660) records became more abundant but do not really contain much biographical information of officers and men which is of use to the researcher until the nineteenth century.

A useful guide for those interested in military records is a recent Public Record Office publication entitled *Records of Officers and Soldiers who have served in the British Army*, published in 1984. For those who have served since 1914 you should consult the Army Records Centre, Bourne Avenue, Hayes, Middlesex UB3 1RS. For those who served in the Royal Artillery, information can be got from the RA Record and Manning Office, Imphal Barracks, York YO1 4HD. Additional information can be obtained from the National Army Museum, Royal Hospital Road, London SW3 4HT, and from the Army Museums Ogilby Trust, Ministry of Defence (Army), 85 Whitehall, London SW1A 2NP. In addition, most regiments have their own museums, some of which contain useful archives.

Officers

Service records of commissioned officers of the British Army can be traced with only approximate completeness from the year 1660. From the mid-eighteenth century preliminary details can be obtained from Army Lists but family details can be found to be only satisfactory if the officer was serving after 1829. There are the Commander-in-Chief's memorandum papers which begin in 1793. Frankly this is over-emphasized as a useful source. Sometimes you can find a letter of recommendation containing family background but experience shows this is the exception rather than the rule. There are returns of officers' service 1808–10, but these give no personal details and only include the ranks of General down to Major.

In 1829 systematic records of services were introduced which were arranged by regiments and these unfortunate officers, of which there were many, were placed on half pay. Both they and their counterparts in the Royal Navy suffered because of the vast reduction of the armed services after the Napoleonic Wars. These records contain place of birth, details of service career, details of marriage, spouse and children, if any, with their dates of birth. You should be able to find such records up to about 1870. Thereafter one has to rely on Army Lists.

Other Ranks

Here you can be more hopeful. The first source one recommends are the soldier discharge papers which cover the years from 1756 to 1913. These are useful only if your man was discharged on a pension, not if he died on active service or if he deserted. Equally it is necessary to know the name of the regiment in which he served until 1873. From then until 1883 the papers are arranged separately for the cavalry, infantry, artillery, and so on. It is only from then onwards you find all discharge certificates, except for those who died, in one long alphabetical series for the whole Army.

These papers contain much information: the place of birth, the age of the soldier when he enlisted, his physical description, previous occupation and intended place of residence on discharge. They also give details of his career and conduct. Furthermore, some show medical details which can be very illuminating especially if he was somewhat intemperate or committed an indiscretion and suffered accordingly. Some of the later papers go even further by giving traces of next of kin, of marriage and of children.

Other series which give you vital information are the Regimental Description Books, whose survival is somewhat precarious, and the Casualty Returns. If all else fails you can search the Muster Rolls and trace a man's activities month by month. Sometimes here you can find personal details. For example, a search was made to find one James Ashley in a certain infantry regiment. There was no Record of Service for him and the Description Book was missing. After a fifteen-year search in the Muster Rolls it was discovered that he and his wife died in a yellow fever epidemic in Bermuda. This disaster occurred as the disease spread from a prison hulk moored off the Island where it began and thereupon it raged all around. His two orphans were sent back to England and put into the Duke of York's Military School. They stayed there for just over a year before they were sent to a maternal uncle in Australia. The reader will be left in no doubt that to find this information was a triumph.

Militia

This ancient body is best described as a part-time army raised when needed. Today it is best known as the Territorial Army. The first series of Muster Rolls dates from 1522–1640. Some of these records are to be found in the Public Record Office, others in private muniments, others still in County Record Offices. You are likely to get information on names only but even that is helpful in this period. A number of these Muster Rolls have been published by local record societies.

The Militia was very active during the Napoleonic Wars when a large part of the regular army was abroad. Most recent records that have survived are in the form of Muster Rolls as described above, but there are some other records.

Royal Flying Corps and Royal Air Force

Although the RFC was part of the Army before and during the First World War, RAF records date from the service's foundation at the end of that war. Some early records are at the Public Record Office in the Paymaster General's Records and among those of the Air Ministry and Foreign Office. In the main, however, they can be obtained from RAF Personnel Management Centre, Eastern Avenue, Barnwood, Gloucester GL4 7AN. RFC records are at the Army Records Centre at Hayes, Middlesex, with possible extra information from the Imperial War Museum, Duxford, Cambridgeshire, and the Air Force Museum at Hendon.

Mercantile Marine

The whole of the merchant service was controlled by the Department of the Board of Trade and under this body was the Registrar General of Shipping and Seamen whose records we are concerned with. Those of genealogical interest begin for seamen who served after 1835. Although from 1747 Masters or owners of ships were obliged to keep Muster Rolls of each voyage made, in which were entered the names of officers and seamen, only a few of these survive up to 1835 when a new system known as 'The Agreements and Crew Lists' was introduced. In the first series, 1835–1844, you can find details of age and place of birth only. The next series, 1845–1853, when the system of seamen's tickets was introduced, is the only one of real value. Here you find place and date of birth, with physical descriptions and the nicety as to whether the seaman could read or write together with his shore residence.

The ticketing system proved so unpopular with seamen and the administration involved outweighed the information gained so it was abolished in October 1853. Thus a new register was introduced, but in 1856 the department was satisfied that the Crew Lists sufficed and that, too, was abolished. Thereafter, unless you know a man's ship together with its port of origin, you will have a difficult task in tracing him.

For Master Mariners and Mates, Certificates of Competency were issued as a result of the Merchant Ship Act of 1850. These registers contain the place and date of birth and the port where the certificate was issued. You should find your man here if he was certificated before 1900.

All the above records are at the Public Record Office, Kew. From 1857 the system changed, so check what is available at Kew and what may be at the National Maritime Museum, Greenwich. For further information about ordinary seamen after 1870 and officers after 1913 you should contact the Registrar General of Shipping and Seamen, Llantrisant Road, Llandaff, Cardiff CF5 2YS.

Customs and Excise

The Boards of Customs and Excise were not amalgamated until 1910. The Customs were responsible for controlling the revenue at ports and the Excise men were responsible for seeing duties were paid.

Some personal details of Customs officers can be found, but records for many at the ports of London and Liverpool have been destroyed.

For Excise men there is a magnificent collection of Board Minute Books dating from 1688 that continue up to the late nineteenth century. From these we can trace a man's career from when he started as a supernumerary until his discharge or death. Often we find that a man followed in his father's footsteps and his own sons followed suit. There are also some entry papers which give personal details of men who joined the services after 1820.

Railwaymen

A railway enthusiast can have a beanfeast at the Public Record Office where he can find a multitude of original records together with many printed histories and periodicals. This mass of stuff deals with every aspect of railway organization which varied from company to company, particularly when it comes to staff records. Regarding the staff records, their usefulness varies and to search them can be frustrating. One only has to use them when you lose a railwayman in records like the Census Returns. Railwaymen obviously were moved about. Often if you are looking for an engine driver in one company you find only the station staff records have survived or vice versa. However, do not be daunted by this and have a go at them if you feel fit to do so. With these records you will also find some for the Inland Waterways. Bargemen and their families are usually elusive to say the least.

The General Post Office

Anyone who is looking for a postmaster or letter carrier, which a postman was formerly known as, can go to the General Post Office record room in London to see what he can find. There are registers of correspondence to look at as well as other material which is interesting, if not biographical. Often you can find reference to a particular person in one form or another. However, searching in this area is not particularly productive.

All the service records listed above, apart from those to do with the postal services who retain their own records, are housed in the Public Record Office at Kew.

Professions and Trades

If your ancestor did belong to one of the professions or trades, it does not necessarily mean that you are going to have an easy path in tracing him, though it is worth taking up the challenge. Before describing the cross-section, it is recommended that you make one or two reference checks in printed sources. The first of these is to consult the University Alumni. Most ancient Universities have published details of their former students back to the sixteenth century. In England there are two publications, namely the Oxford and Cambridge Alumni. The details you will find in these records are the names of the father, his rank and occupation, where the student lived, his college and his later career if known.

If you fail here you can try the Dublin Alumni, and following this, the printed books of the four old Scottish Universities. Sometimes one can be very lucky in one's searches of these records and find whole generations of families.

Many public schools, too, have published records which can be consulted.

Clergy

Practically all clergy of the Church of England in former years went to either Oxford or Cambridge. The famous *Crockford's* was first published in 1848. Before this date there were Clergy Lists as well as ordination papers which are kept in the diocesan office of the See in which the priest was ordained.

You will find records of the Nonconformist clergymen among the records of their particular denominations. However, the best place to start is to look at a card index in the Dr Williams Library in London which gives you details of mainly Independent and Congregational clergymen. These usually give some details of their background and you can sometimes find their photograph and references to their funeral sermons as well. Similarly for a Baptist minister you go to the Baptist Union where again they have their own card index. For Methodists and others there are details at the John Rylands Library in Manchester.

Medical Profession

Early material concerning doctors is really rather sketchy. There are a few records at the libraries of the Royal Colleges of Physicians and Surgeons. Curiously enough few doctors went to English universities. They were trained either in Edinburgh or at Leyden in Holland.

The first medical directory was published in 1847 and in 1849 a system of medical registration was set up. The entries show their qualifications and the place where they were practising. They may have been members of the Barber Surgeons' Company or members of the Society of Apothecaries. In 1815 licenciates of the latter society were introduced which cover apothecaries all over the country. Today we think of apothecaries as pharmacists or chemists but at that time practically all doctors would have had that qualification. Looking at the records you will see that the courses they attended covered a much wider area than basic chemistry.

Legal Professions

Barristers when called to the Bar became members of one of the four Inns of Court. They all have published records of their members. If you want further information you can always apply to the library of the particular Inn. For solicitors and attorneys there are Law Lists. To find more detailed information there are also indentures at the Public Record Office for men who were attached to the Court of Common Pleas and the King's Bench.

Apprenticeship

Apprenticeship for trades and professions dates back in some cases to the Middle Ages. Livery Companies and Guilds were formed particularly in the city of London and in some of the major trading cities such as Bristol, Exeter, York and Newcastle. They laid down standards of workmanship for their craft. As a result young men were bound to masters of the trade concerned for periods varying from five to nine years after which they became freemen of the company.

Many of these records have survived and for London many have been deposited at the Guildhall Library while others are still in the Halls of the companies concerned, e.g. the Goldsmiths' and Stationers' companies, where you can apply direct for information. Similar records exist for the provincial guilds.

The apprentice binding registers usually give the name, address and trade of the apprentice and address of the master. Besides being apprenticed it was possible to become a freeman of a company by redemption which meant that you paid a fee having satisfied the Livery of your capabilities.

If you are not sure to which company your ancestor belonged, you are encouraged to go in person to the City Chamberlain's office to search the freedoms admission register, or failing this, apply in writing.

It is important to note that from the beginning of the nineteenth century a man could belong to a company different from that of his trade, i.e. a fishmonger could belong to the Drapers' Company.

Besides these sources there is an index of details of Apprentices compiled by Perceval Boyd from Inland Revenue records, copies of which are kept at the Society of Genealogists and the Guildhall Library. This is presented in two series, namely 1710–1760 and 1761–1772. Between the latter date and 1809 you can wade through the registers in the Public Record Office which are unindexed. These do not include poor law apprentices which are mentioned in Chapter 4.

Records of the British in India

There is a considerable collection of personal records of the East India Company and later of the Indian Empire at the India Record Office and library. This contains details of the Civil Service and the Army, as well as other personnel living in the subcontinent.

For those interested in Indian Service Records of the Honourable East India Company or the Indian Army, application should be made to the India Office Library and Records, 197 Blackfriars Road, London SE1 8NG, but the records of the regular Army in India are with the other Army records at the Public Record Office, Kew.

CHAPTER TEN
Celtic Ancestors

The inhabitants of Cornwall and Wales, as well as of Scotland and Ireland, were Celtic rather than Anglo-Saxon. As in the early 1800s half the population of the British Isles lived in these areas it is an important aspect, and family history in these areas has some particular features as a result of the racial background. The first is surnames: all of the Celtic races originally used 'patronymics' rather than surnames, which means that in place of a surname they used their father's and/or their grandfather's christian names.

So for example, a Welshman called 'Evan ap Llewellyn ap Owen' was Evan son of Llewellyn, son of Owen, and Cornishmen would use the same formula, but without the 'ap', so a Cornishman named John Richard William was John son of Richard son of William. In the course of time these became fixed as regular surnames – generally earlier at higher social levels and in the less remote areas, and later among poorer people and in remoter areas. So a squire in Monmouthshire or East Cornwall would have adopted a fixed surname before 1600, but a labourer near Lands End or in Snowdonia could be found using a patronymic name in the 1750s. Mostly these became fixed as surnames simply as Williams, Jones (John), etc. But some Welsh names slurred the 'ap' so that 'ap Richard' became 'Prichard', and similarly Prees or Price, Proger, Bowen and Bevan derive from ap Rhys, ap Roger, ap Owen and ap Evan.

In Scotland and Ireland it worked similarly but the Gaelic language gave them 'Mac' for 'son of' and (only in Ireland) 'Ui or 'O' for 'grandson of', and so you get the numerous names beginning in 'Mac' and 'O'. But these were further complicated by the clan system so that not only would everyone descending from the original Donald call themselves MacDonald, but others who joined the clan would as well, although not related. The Scots tended to keep their prefix 'Mac', but quite often the Irish have dropped the 'O' in more recent years. For example, President Ronald Reagan's great-grandfather in County Tipperary began his life as

Michael O'Regan. The Scots and the Irish began using fixed surnames earlier than the Welsh or Cornish.

As well as the clan system, genealogy was important to the Celts for inheritance of their land. Welshmen for example, inherited land by 'gavelkind', equal shares for each child, and so preserved their genealogies as title deeds to their lands. For many people from kings to abbots and minor chieftains, their position depended upon their kinship as much as it did for small farmers. As a result there is a great deal of genealogy preserved from very early dates; the O'Neills of Ulster have the most ancient documented pedigree in Western Europe, and there is the saying 'as long as a Welsh pedigree'.

Nor should it be thought that these ancient pedigrees are out of reach of ordinary people. A minor Scottish customs official has been traced back to Ailill Olum, King of Munster in Ireland, one and a half millennia before, and President Ronald Reagan is a great-great-grandson of Thomas O'Regan, a poor landless labourer who none the less descends from Raigan, nephew of the great King Brian Boru, a thousand years before.

But all too often, Celtic genealogy gets lost in the confusion of too many people with a single surname, with inadequate records to distinguish who is who, Jones and Davies in Wales, Williams and Thomas in Cornwall, MacDonald and Campbell in Scotland, Murphy and O'Brien in Ireland. There is a glen in the Scottish Highlands where every family was surnamed Ross, and a hundred and thirty-two Ryan families in a single village in Tipperary. Add to this the problem, all too often, of laxity in keeping more recent records, and the common problem of Celtic genealogy is to bridge the gap between nineteenth- and twentieth-century records and the earlier traditional pedigrees.

Some of the paucity of records is due to causes like the Hebrideans who kept no parish registers as firstly, everyone knew everyone's family history anyway, so why write it down? and secondly, few if any of them could read or write. Oral family history is important, for many old people can remember traditions of families, often surprisingly far back. One man's grandmothers, one Irish, one Scottish, gave him a great deal of the story of his ancestors, and the intense interest that Celts have in their own and their neighbours' ancestors is surprising until you remember it is a habit ingrained for a thousand years and more.

It is important to remember that the Celts had their own languages, Irish and Scottish Gaelic, Welsh and (now extinct) Cornish. Only the earlier records are written in these languages, but a trap is when surnames are Anglicized, for example when the Scottish or Irish 'Gowan' and Cornish 'Gof' get translated as Smith. Apart from these aspects the records for more recent Welsh and Cornish research are organized in the English way, as described in earlier chapters. Welsh archives are divided between the National Library of Wales at Aberystwyth, and local county record offices. As the latter are a new development, the National Library remains the key source, and they have there as well a treasure-house of ancient Welsh genealogies.

In Scotland, the archives are ideally organized. The parish registers of the (Presbyterian) Church of Scotland were all called in to the central archives in 1855, and this coincides with the start of Scottish General Registration on 1 January 1855. There are also census records open to the public up to 1891.

Nearly all the Scottish archives a family historian will need are very conveniently in the two adjoining buildings of the Scottish Record Office and the West Register House in Edinburgh. In addition to the usual sources of General Registration, parish registers, wills (called 'testaments' in Scotland) and census records, there is a further vast series of records unique in Europe, which reflect the fact that the Law of Scotland is based upon Roman Law rather than upon the Common Law of England, Ireland and America. These records are legal ones, relating particularly to the ownership, inheritance and acquisition of land, of which the most important are 'Services of Heirs' and 'Sasines'. Since in Scotland, land could not be devised by a will but could only pass by either inheritance or by legal act, a great deal of the genealogy of any owners of land and their relations is recorded in these archives. In general the wealth of material available in Edinburgh means that researching Scottish family history should be a happy task.

Irish research is, however, a subject on its own, but an important one, as in 1801 one-third of the population of the British Isles lived in Ireland. To understand Irish research one needs to understand Irish history. The truly Irish people have ancient roots in their country, and this is the race to whom much of Europe is indebted for a legacy of Christianity and culture.

In the Middle Ages, Anglo-Norman knights invaded Ireland and became assimilated – 'more Irish than the Irish themselves'. Burke, for example, is the Norman name de Burgo. Later settlers in Ireland were Protestant, as distinct from the ancient race which was, and has mostly remained, Roman Catholic. From England came the so-called 'Anglo-Irish' landowners, merchants, and the like; from Scotland came Presbyterians who largely settled in the northern Irish province of Ulster – these being usually termed in America the 'Scotch-Irish'. There were other much smaller groups too, such as the Huguenots from France and the Palatines from Germany. In the later seventeenth and for much of the eighteenth centuries, Penal Laws repressed the Catholics, and most power and wealth was represented by the 'Protestant Ascendancy' of the Anglo-Irish. As a result, early Catholic church registers are rare, and they left few other records as they could not, for example, legally own land.

The difficulties of Irish research tend to be exaggerated, because the Public Record Office at the Four Courts in Dublin was burnt down in 1922, and much of what was there was lost. However, it has to be appreciated that only about half the existing Church of Ireland (Protestant Episcopal) parish registers were lost in the fire – and the majority of those were from small rural parishes with few Protestant inhabitants, while seven-eighths of the population were Catholic or Presbyterian, whose parish registers were not in the record office in 1922, and so were not lost. Certainly the original probate court records were also lost, but a great many of these wills survive as copies or in the abstracts. The general question of Irish research is governed by the scattered nature of the records, which is in many ways a blessing as this saved them from loss in 1922.

Northern Ireland, six counties in the province of Ulster, became separate in 1922, and many local records are held there, but as Dublin was the capital of all of Ireland until that date, some important archives relating to the North are still in Dublin. For example, one such treasury of information is at the Registry of Deeds at King's Inn in Dublin where all property deeds and records such as wills relating to property are recorded (much like an American county courthouse, but with all thirty-two counties recorded together) after 1708, and at the Genealogical Office in Dublin Castle there are the recorded pedigrees of many of the Anglo-Irish landowners and their families.

General Registration of births, marriages and deaths in Ireland began on 1 January 1864 (although registration of Protestant marriages began in 1845) and copies of the Dublin registrations relating to the Northern six counties are held in Belfast. Parish registers of all denominations for the six counties, or microfilms of them, are also either held in the Public Record Office of Northern Ireland, Belfast, or are being gathered in.

In the twenty-six counties of the South, the Republic of Ireland, records of General Registration are kept at the Custom House, Dublin. For parish registers it is much more complicated: Catholic registers (which relate to the great majority of the population) are held by the individual parish priests, but microfilms of all of these prior to 1880 are at the National Library in Dublin – although the written permission of the respective priest is necessary before they can be examined. Church of Ireland registers are largely still held by the rectors of each parish, although increasingly the registers, or copies or microfilms of them, are being deposited at the Public Record Office in Dublin. Quaker records are kept at the Friends' Meeting House in Eustace Street, Dublin. Other important archives in Dublin are held by Trinity College, the State Paper Office in Dublin Castle, the Representative Body of the Church of Ireland, and for lawyers, the Library at King's Inn. The period before the suppression of native Irish culture in the seventeenth century is superbly documented in the library of the Royal Irish Academy. Finally, it should be remembered that all of Ireland was governed from London before 1922, and many records are in British archives (particularly of the army, navy and police).

In essence, Irish research is not easy, but the difficulties are often exaggerated, and a great deal can be accomplished with care and application. The reward for success can be connection with some of the oldest documented pedigrees in Western Europe.

CHAPTER ELEVEN
Immigrants

Throughout history the British Isles have played host to people from all over Europe, and more recently from all over the world, who wished to settle here. There are many Britons whose parents or grandparents came here as refugees from tyrannical regimes in Europe, the chief of these being Jews, Poles and Russians.

During the eighteenth and nineteenth centuries a few permanent refugees came to Britain, fleeing the French Revolution, and Germans came in the wake of the Hanoverian Kings. From the family historian's point of view one of the largest groups of immigrants were the Huguenots who came in large numbers during the sixteenth and seventeenth centuries, and it is with them that we propose to concern ourselves in this chapter.

The origins of French Protestantism are to be found in the teachings of Erasmus and Luther. As elsewhere in northern Europe it was the availability of printed bibles almost more than anything else which had such a profound effect on the academic, professional and artisan classes of society. The Church reacted vigorously and the faculty of theology of the Sorbonne obtained from François I an ordinance in 1535 for the suppression of printing. However the demand for bibles grew rapidly, and wherever they were read in the vernacular, the movement for reform grew apace.

The Huguenots had been assured that liberty of conscience would be granted, and showed themselves to be loyal subjects on the accession of Louis XIV, when their rights under the Edict of Nantes were reaffirmed. Once Louis XIV gained his majority, persecution began to increase and rights offered by the Edict of Nantes were eroded until its final revocation in 1685. More than 400 proclamations, edicts and declarations attacking the Huguenots in their households, civil freedom, property and liberty of conscience were promulgated between 1660 and 1685, in the course of which time more than 200,000 Huguenots left France to seek sanctuary in Switzerland, Germany, the Netherlands and England.

Owing to the restrictions placed upon their movements by these Edicts, those from south-east France mainly went to Switzerland, seeking the shortest route. Those in the north-east and some from the north-west went to the Netherlands; most from the north-west and south-west came to England. From Normandy, Picardy and the Pas de Calais they arrived in strength in Kent and Sussex. Those using the Atlantic route from Saintonge and Aunis formed the basis of the French Churches in the west of England. However, it did not mean that all would stay at their first port of refuge. Those who eventually settled in Germany travelled via Switzerland, and the American Huguenots mainly descend from those who had at first sought refuge in England. During the last decade of the seventeenth century, when William of Orange was not only Stadtholder of the Netherlands but also King of the United Kingdom, there was a great interchange of refugees between the Netherlands, England and Ireland.

It is always natural that refugees should choose to live near their fellow countrymen, especially where communities exist that have been established as a result of previous migration. Such places in England were London and Canterbury. Some emigrants were close to and used the liturgy of the Church of England, but others were closer to Presbyterian doctrines and were classed as Nonconformists. Between 1681 and 1720 approximately 200,000 Huguenots left France and of these it is thought that some 40,000 came to England and of those, about 15,000 settled in London. This migration, spread over forty years, should be seen in the context of the contemporary population of London in 1700, which was 50,000.

The Huguenots settled in two main London colonies, in Soho and Spitalfields. Spitalfields already had a long tradition of political and religious disaffection, and was a stronghold of nonconformity. The silk weaving industry had already been established there in the first half of the century, so it was a natural rallying point for immigrant Huguenot artisans, particularly those skilled in that industry.

Why Soho became the other great centre is not so clear. It was possibly because the French congregation had settled in that part of Westminster in the 1640s. In 1682, when large scale migration from France began, these refugees were granted a lease of the Greek Chapel in Soho, which no doubt attracted many of them to this quarter of London. It also seems that many who settled in Soho were of bourgeois and aristocratic backgrounds. This is supported by the fact that many of these refugees were goldsmiths or silversmiths, jewellers, engravers, clock and watchmakers, or tapestry weavers, who naturally gravitated to the fashionable residential quarter of London near to the Court.

By the second half of the eighteenth century the specifically Huguenot character of both Soho and Spitalfields had declined greatly. Many of the refugee families had become anglicized through intermarriage and knew nothing of the persecution which had originally brought them from Europe. By 1800 only two Huguenot chapels survived in Soho, but one chapel in Spitalfields was still using the French language in 1840. During this period, the centre of the silk weaving industry moved from Spitalfields to Bethnal Green and this no doubt helped to destroy many of the French influences and ways of life which had been prevalent in Spitalfields. But there remains a French Church in Soho Square to this day.

Huguenot records in France vary according to locality. In the country as a whole there are few which begin before 1660, but those of Caen, La Rochelle, Rouen and Nîmes are very extensive and begin at the end of the sixteenth century and continue up to the Revocation of the Edict of Nantes in 1685. The usefulness of French Protestant records is not confined to English and American families of Huguenot descent. They contain many references to English, Scottish and Irish Protestant families resident in France, and especially to merchants trading between British and French ports.

For those who have Huguenot ancestors, membership of the Huguenot Society is of great value. The society's transactions include transcriptions of all Huguenot parish registers as well as naturalization papers and kindred material. Three books published in 1985, the tercentenary of the Revocation of the Edict of Nantes, are of exceptional importance to those of Huguenot descent. They are *Huguenot Heritage* by Robin Gwynn; *A Family from Flanders* by John Peters; and *Huguenot Ancestry* by Noel Currer-Briggs and Royston Gambier.

The medieval Jewish communities in England (Jews were prominent in Exeter) were expelled in 1290. Small crypto-Jewish communities existed in London and Bristol in the sixteenth century, but due to contemporary persecution they were outwardly Christian and were recorded in Anglican registers. The official readmission of Jews dates from 1655, the earliest being Sephardim from Portugal and Spain who settled in London. Later arrivals were Ashkenazim from Germany and Central Europe (some coming via the British colonies in the West Indies and North America) and it is these who are relevant outside London. The oldest surviving Ashkenazi synagogue in the country is that at Plymouth founded in 1768. Their activities were in specialized trades, for example as jewellers or tailors, or in naval victualling, and international commerce. Jews suffered numerous legal disabilities until the nineteenth century, only being allowed to own property from 1728, have British nationality from 1740, vote in elections from 1835, and graduate at universities from 1870. However, their religion did not bar their wills from the Christian Church probate courts.

Jewish records are a specialized subject on their own. Firstly certain of them are in Hebrew or Yiddish, some using the Hebrew alphabet and the Jewish calendar. Secondly, what is recorded is largely distinct from Christian registers; for example birth records are rare, and commonly there are only registers of circumcision of boys (at eight days old); conversely marriage records are particularly good, often including the marriage contract, despite Jewish marriages being exempted from Lord Hardwicke's Marriage Act of 1753; surnames are a particular difficulty, as these were often changed, and secular surnames may not occur in synagogue records where the patronymic (for example Moses ben Jacob) was used. Wills are a particularly valuable source, and due to a good deal of mobility a large proportion were proved in the Prerogative Court of Canterbury, but many other sources are eliminated by legal disabilities; for example Jews did not have a vote before 1835 so they do not appear in earlier voters lists or poll books.

There are extensive collections of material (including many researched pedigrees) at the Jewish Museum, London, and the Mocatta Library, University College, London. The Wiener Library, holding a great deal of German and other continental material (relevant in so far as nearly all British Jews are of immigrant origin) has been transferred to Tel Aviv. Printed material includes a general guide with a good bibliography: Edgar R. Samuel, *The Jews*, *National Index of*

Parish Registers, III (Chichester 1974), pp. 957–976. There are extensive references in the *Proceedings of the Jewish Historical Society*, (in progress); and in Cecil Roth's *The Rise of Provincial Jewry* (1950). Since most Jews in England are of immigrant origins, the extensive material on aliens at the Public Record Office, London, particularly in classes HO 1 to HO 4, is invaluable.

CHAPTER TWELVE
Emigration

North America

For an American of European descent, the attempt to identify emigrant ancestors requires much preliminary work in America before searches can be undertaken profitably in Europe. He must discover when his ancestor's name first appears in American records; who were the emigrant's closest associates; whether he was a trapper, planter or professional man; to what religious or ethnic group he belonged; whether he remained in one city or state all his life; whether his children married within the local community or outside it; if he was a man of property – can any clue to his origin be gained from knowing the name he gave his home or plantation; to whom was he related by blood and marriage. These and other seemingly trivial questions must be answered before one can hope to identify him in Europe. Furthermore, the problem of finding these answers varies from state to state and from one century to another; thus a knowledge of how the states of America were settled is essential.

North America from the Gulf of Mexico to the Arctic has been populated by migrants who arrived over a period of nearly four hundred years beginning in the late sixteenth century. Broadly speaking, those who settled on the eastern coastal plains between latitudes thirty-five degrees and fifty degrees north were English, Dutch, Scandinavian and French in origin. At first they occupied a fairly narrow belt of land bounded in the west by the Appalachians and the Great Lakes. South of thirty-five degrees, which embraces Florida and the West Indies, the settlements were mainly Spanish, interspersed with settlements of French, Dutch and English. The Mississippi valley was a French preserve, west of which ranged the vast Spanish empire of Central America, consisting not only of modern Mexico and all the states to its south-east, but also Texas and California as far north as latitude forty degrees. Not until the nineteenth century was the remainder of the landmass settled by Europeans in a movement of population which continues today.

Within this huge area of space and time, the pattern and rate of migration has been regulated by economic, political and religious factors, operating not only within Europe itself, but also within its individual countries and their provinces. Migration is hardly ever a matter of free, unfettered choice; there are always factors that drive as well as attract. To the well-to-do, America has offered opportunities to the enterprising. To the less well off it promised land and work; to the poor, the petty criminal and the member of unpopular minorities, there was virtually no choice, unless it were one between death or prison at home and exile abroad. During the past two hundred years, however, most European migrants have gone to America under some kind of duress. By contrast, the promoters of the London Virginia Company proclaimed in 1610 the advantages of colonization and emigration as being three in number: first, to preach Christianity to the pagan natives; second, to relieve overcrowding at home; and, lastly, to obtain fruitful land on which to grow products for export to Europe.

To settle colonies you need not only leaders but labourers and the motives of those who commanded were very different from those who had to obey. So the attraction of America to the French Huguenot or English Brownist was quite different from that which motivated the Dutch or English merchant. Genealogists, therefore, must be aware of such differences when they attempt to identify particular emigrants. Because most emigrants were from humble stations in life, and because, in England especially, there were numerous people bearing identical names, it is probable that identification will only be by means of circumstantial, rather than direct, evidence.

British settlement in North America began very simply. Various groups settled along the northern half of the east coast – now essentially in what is known as New England – and along the southern coast to the north of Florida. This area was loosely termed Virginia, a far wider area than the modern state of that name.

Contrary to general popular belief, North America was not first colonized by the passengers who sailed in the *Mayflower* in 1620. The earliest permanent colony was founded at

Jamestown, in Virginia, in 1607. The main impetus to settlement came from the pressure of primogeniture (whereby the eldest son inherited the lion's share of the family property) upon younger sons of the landed, merchant and professional classes. Much of the early labour force came as indentured servants through the ports of Bristol and London, and quite a few records survive of their names and the length of time they had to serve. The southern states operated the 'headright' system, whereby anyone who paid the fare of a passenger to people the colony was entitled to a grant of fifty acres of land. Although there were cases of abuse, the system generated lists of persons arriving in the colony, a source of great value if you understand that the date of a grant supported by such a list could often mean that those whose names appear on it came several years earlier. The richer planters would purchase headrights as well as claim them for passengers they had brought themselves, and in the case of some of the larger plantations, these lists run to several hundred names collected over as long a period as ten to twelve years.

New England, on the other hand, was largely colonized by groups of religious dissidents. There was, for example, a Cambridge-based Puritan group, drawing members from as far away as Yorkshire and Kent; groups based on Dorchester, Plymouth and to a lesser extent on Bristol. These were attracted as much by the fine cod-fisheries as by the chance to practise their religion freely. The origins of many of these immigrants can be traced by identifying the group to which they belonged, though it has to be emphasized that, being religious in character, they attracted members from all over the country. On the other hand, those who exported indentured servants to Virginia usually recruited them in their home districts, so it is important to establish from where in England the planter who claimed the headright came before starting to look for the places of origin of his servants.

It is obviously impossible to cover this large subject in a short chapter such as this, but groups of intermarried kin from south Yorkshire, East Anglia, Kent and London can be identified, and colonies like Maryland (Catholic) and Pennsylvania (Quaker) offer clues to where searches should be started.

With these differences in mind, it is easy to understand why the northern colonies in the seventeenth century attracted men and women from all over Britain, for their common interest was a dislike of the Established Church. This means that the genealogist must search among sectarian records rather than among the archives of a particular region, though even in New England, and particularly in Massachusetts, the majority emigrated from the south-east of England through the port of London.

The English Civil Wars of the 1640s completely changed the pattern of migration. Virginia remained loyal to the King, whereas New England supported parliament. For the first time in its history Virginia began to welcome political refugees, not only from England, but also from other transatlantic colonies. The Civil Wars ended the trading monopoly of London, and thereafter Bristol began to trade in tobacco and sugar from the Americas and to export indentured servants to the colonies. Between 1654 and 1685 the names of more than 10,000 indentured servants are to be found in the Bristol records destined for Virginia and the West Indies. During the same period, emigration to New England almost dried up completely. With this shift in the pattern of trade from London to Bristol, the recruiting ground for emigrants switched from the south-east to the Severn valley, South Wales and those regions of Wiltshire, Somerset and Dorset lying within a radius of fifty miles of Bristol.

It is a common, though erroneous, belief that once an emigrant left Europe he never returned. There is also a belief that if a name is found, say, in Barbados, it cannot possibly belong to an individual of the same name living in Virginia or New England at about the same time. While it is indeed true to say that the majority of emigrants stayed where they were once they arrived on the far side of the Atlantic, nevertheless, mobility between one colony and another, as well as back and forth across the ocean, was by no means rare, or confined to the rich, to seamen or to traders. There are numerous instances of men and women of modest means, even of servants, returning home to visit relatives or to attend to family business, in particular to matters connected with the inheritance of property.

Even though emigration in the earliest years was on the

whole voluntary, nevertheless forced transportation as a punishment began as early as 1615. It has been estimated that more than 30,000 convicts were transported from England to America and the West Indies between that date and 1775. (See *English Convicts in Colonial America* by P. W. Coldham, 1983.)

The southern and northern fringes each have different histories. The Trustees of Georgia, who founded that colony in 1732, were a group of philanthropists who sought to found a colony for debtors. Nova Scotia, on the other hand, was set up as an outpost against the French in Canada and settled largely by Scots. (For a more thorough exploration of this complicated question see T. C. C. Graham's *Colonists from Scotland, 1707–1783* 1981, E. G. Hartman's *Emigration from Wales* 1967, and N. Currer-Briggs's *Worldwide Family History* 1982.)

Canada

Canada, as is generally known, was colonized by the French in the seventeenth century. Following the independence of the United States, Canada became the only British possession on the North American mainland. By 1791 six provinces had come into existence: Lower Canada, the most populous and longest settled, was overwhelmingly French; Upper Canada and New Brunswick had only just been created; the settlement of Prince Edward Island (formerly St John Island) had barely begun; Newfoundland and Nova Scotia were older British possessions. The British population of Canada differed radically from that of the thirteen colonies which had seceded. Many loyalists had fled from them to avoid persecution at the hands of American radicals, which meant that they were not only staunchly royalist but also very conservative.

Comparatively few settlers arrived in Canada before 1814, but by 1851 more than 200,000 English-speaking Americans had come to the north bank of the St Lawrence and of Lakes Ontario and Erie and to the eastern shore of Lake Huron. (For further information see *Canada – A Political and Social History* by E. McMinnis, 1985.)

Australia and New Zealand

European settlement here has taken place only in the last two centuries, and owes a good deal to the aftermath of the

American Revolution. It was first suggested as somewhere the dispossessed Loyalists could be settled, but a greater attraction for the British Government was the fact that Australia was a place to which the convicts, who would formerly have been sent to Virginia and Maryland and who were overcrowding British prisons, could be transported.

So Australia began as a penal settlement when the First Fleet landed at Sydney Cove on 26 January 1788, carrying 736 convicts and 294 officers and men to govern and guard them. For the first two decades, the new arrivals were largely convicts, with a few 'gentleman settlers', often former Army officers. Transportation of convicts did not cease until 1868, but by 1820 New South Wales was no longer solely a penal settlement, and the wool trade, soon to be the mainstay of the country's economy, had begun. 200,000 free settlers arrived between 1820 and 1850 almost entirely from the British Isles, with a sprinkling of Germans. The Gold Rush began in 1851, and this led to the population trebling in thirty years. Australian emigration can be put into perspective when we learn that it was not until about 1870 that native-born Australians outnumbered immigrants, and the British and Irish element in their origins did not fall below 95 per cent until 1945. In New Zealand there was no penal settlement, and little immigration before the 1840s; the major influx came after the discovery of gold in 1861, and the proportion of British and Irish ancestry in the make-up of New Zealanders is even higher than in that of Australians.

From the family historian's point of view, the importance of this is that most of his ancestors left the British Isles in the era of modern records and they were already recorded there in civil registration of births, marriages and deaths, and in the census. In addition to this, the new colonies (as they were then) began keeping good records of their own. Not only did they introduce civil registration earlier than most European and American states, but they recorded a great deal of detail about the family, which is hard to equal anywhere else in the world as a working tool for genealogists. Jeremiah Sullivan's death certificate is a classic example, and shows why no one should search for an Australian's or a New Zealander's emigrant origins without every effort being made first to find these records.

Civil registration of this type began in New Zealand in 1848, and in Australia at various dates: Tasmania 1838, Western Australia and Victoria 1841, South Australia 1842, New South Wales and Queensland 1856. Before those dates, there are church registers of baptisms, marriages and burials; there are also tombstones which supply information, but these are neither as complete nor as informative as civil registration records, although Norfolk Island church registers, for example, date back to 1790. As is inevitable in a developing country, and because people are only human, not every event was recorded: a death was registered by someone who got the facts wrong, or a priest performing a marriage failed to enter all of the answers on the printed form, but most Australians and New Zealanders can trace their ancestry back through registration of births, marriages and deaths to a specific place and date in the British Isles, simply from the Registrars' records, without any great difficulty. This is particularly true of those whose ancestors emigrated in the 1850s or later, although, of course, many of the earlier settlers died after civil registration had begun, and it should not be forgotten that their death certificates carry the same information.

Those who slipped through the net of the system for one reason or another, as well as earlier arrivals, present more problems. They can be classified in two groups: those who arrived as convicts and those who came as free settlers – although the two groups tend to be confused by the fact that a number of convicts' wives and families emigrated as free settlers to join their men.

In general, and perhaps ironically, the early free settlers are harder to trace than the convicts. Passenger lists of departures at the British end do not usually survive from before 1890, but Australian and New Zealand passenger arrival lists are very extensive, and *should* record families with their ages and 'native places'. They are generally classified by ship's name and by date, and many have been indexed, but for those that have not more information is needed, as without these two facts the sheer physical task of searching the vast lists is daunting. Fortunately a lot of earlier Australian records include this information, notably censuses and Immigration Agents' lists. There was a series of censuses of New South Wales and Tasmania, some of which listed the convict population only, and others the free population as well, of which the most complete is that of 1828. British army records can help as well, not only for the men originally sent out as garrisons and guards for the convicts, but also for those who emigrated under a government scheme to encourage army pensioners to settle there.

Convict ancestry is no disgrace in Australia; indeed there is an exclusive club in Melbourne of which membership is limited to those with such a forebear, and an Australian takes as much pride in an ancestor on the First Fleet as does an American whose ancestor was on the *Mayflower*, but with the advantage that Australian convicts are better documented.

In terms of the technicalities of research, Australian records such as censuses, permits to marry, tickets of leave and the like usually identify convicts either by the ship they were carried in and the date of arrival, or by the date and place of conviction in Britain or Ireland. From these records, or from the Transportation Registers (which are arranged by date and indexed by ship) one can discover the Assizes or other court where the prisoner was sentenced. The reference to date and place of conviction is important, as the court records are so vast that it would be otherwise all but impossible to find the correct entry.

The court record of the crime (usually a petty one) including the evidence and conviction is usually a piece of family history in itself, even if it is not a particularly happy chapter. Often there is very little evidence in court of the birthplace of the prisoner, and naturally a great many crimes were committed away from home anyway. Of course, you can get examples like the trial of Charles Fancoat in Scotland, 1854, the record of which runs for 117 pages. Among the witnesses who appeared in testimony of his character was the clergyman from the parish 250 miles away in Staffordshire, where he had been born. More often, however, it is necessary to follow the chain of bureaucracy which comes into being after conviction and sentence, and which no legal system seems able to avoid. London is very well served with the records of the Newgate Calendar and the Old Bailey Sessions, as well as Criminal Registers starting in 1791. For the rest of the country Criminal Registers start in 1805, and list all persons charged with crimes, the outcome of the trial and the sentence. Prison records list convicts held both in prisons and in the hulks awaiting transportation; from there they can be followed through to the Transportation Registers. Usually at one or more points in the sequence of records the important facts of the age and birthplace of the convict are recorded, as well as their state of health, their behaviour and other personal details. Most of these records are in the Public Record Office in London, although records of trials in Scotland and Ireland or English county quarter sessions are in the respective national or county record offices. Many of the major records are available on microfilm in Australia.

South Africa

Europeans have lived in South Africa for more than four hundred years. If the arrival of the Portuguese is taken as a starting point, European Africa has a history as long as that of Latin America; if, on the other hand, one takes the Dutch occupation of Table Bay as the beginning, South Africa has a history almost as long as that of the United States. For the purposes of this book, however, the British occupation of the lands south of the Zambezi is what concerns us. (See also E. A. Walker's *History of South Africa* 1957, and N. Currer-Briggs's *Worldwide Family History* 1982.)

The first British occupation of the Cape lasted from 1795 to 1803. At that time there were some 16,000 Europeans. This period was followed by the brief rule of the Batavian Republic (1803–6) before the second British occupation which lasted till 1823. In common with the United States, Canada, Australia and New Zealand, South Africa took its share of immigrants during the late nineteenth century and early twentieth, the reasons being the same as those which prompted migration to these other countries.

The Union of South Africa was formed in 1910, and the country left the Commonwealth in 1961. Genealogical research in South Africa is comparatively easy due to the small European population of the country before 1820, when there were only 43,000 settlers, 9,000 of whom lived in or near Cape Town. The three northern provinces of Transvaal, Natal and the Orange Free State were not opened up until the Great Trek of 1838. The first uniform law for the registration of births, deaths and marriages for the whole of South Africa was in 1923. Before 1921 each republic/colony/province had its own legislation. (See *Worldwide Family History* pp 196–206 for addresses and details of relevant legislation.)

CHAPTER THIRTEEN
Heraldry and Family History

A basic knowledge of the principles of heraldry and of the somewhat archaic way in which arms are described is useful for those in search of their ancestry. In fact, much of heraldry can be described as pictorial genealogy, for its main purpose is to do with identification and inheritance. There is probably more nonsense and misunderstanding about heraldry than about any other aspect of genealogy and family history. Its value to the researcher is firstly to identify an individual or his immediate connections, and then to place him into the appropriate slot in a pedigree.

The origins of heraldry date from the eleventh century and arose from the need for personal identification on the battlefield and through the use of seals on legal documents. The emblems adopted for shield and seal were handed down from father to son over generations and thus became an integral part of each family's history. Shields are still used by companies and corporate bodies though almost never by individuals.

In order to introduce some order into the assumption, granting and registering of arms, colleges of heralds arose, who worked on behalf of the sovereign who was generally recognized as the fount of honour. The heralds were given power to settle disputes and to legalize grants of arms and to make new grants. Every coat of arms must first have been granted, or, if it had been assumed before the institution of the College of Arms, have been recognized by, or on behalf of the sovereign, and its transmission or destination (usually in the male line) follows that set out in the original patent or confirmation, just like most hereditary titles. In Scotland, only the eldest son inherits his father's arms, but all younger sons have the right to matriculate a differenced version of their paternal arms. Thus someone of the same surname as you has no more right to bear your family's arms than someone named Howard has the right to call himself Duke of Norfolk.

Most people think of heraldry as something exclusive to the nobility and gentry. In practice, however, it is not like this at all. The junior branches of some noble houses have over the space of four or five generations fallen on hard times and sunk in the social scale. Many new families have risen from humble origins and applied for grants of arms in the recent past. Social mobility, therefore, ensures that heraldry is widely disseminated.

The two main categories of importance to genealogists are familial and individual heraldry. The former is practised throughout Europe, and we shall be saying a little about continental heraldry below. Familial heraldry pertains to a family rather than to an individual, whereby all male descendants of the original grantee bear the same family arms undifferenced, in much the same way as all the children of a Count of the Holy Roman Empire, for example, would be counts and countesses themselves. Such a system is only practical where there are a great many surnames, though it is a mistake to believe that there is a coat of arms for every surname.

The College of Arms in London is responsible for all aspects of English and Welsh heraldry and for much of Irish and Commonwealth heraldry too. Many Americans apply to the College for coats of arms or the right to bear the arms of families from whom they are descended. It is an independent and semi-private body of kings of arms, heralds and pursuivants responsible to the sovereign through the Earl Marshal.

Individual heraldry, as the name implies, means that an individual is granted a unique coat of arms which allude to factors such as his position in the family, ownership of fiefs, baronies or other titles, or as happens in Spain and Portugal, his four grandparental quarterings can be marshalled together. By its very nature, individual heraldry is therefore of much help to the genealogist.

In Scotland individual heraldry is seen at its best. The high proportion of its nobility to the total population, the clan system and the relatively small number of surnames, its feudal system of land tenure and the precision of the Scottish temperament, have encouraged people to know their relative position vis-à-vis their clan chiefs. These tendencies are vividly illustrated by the large attendances at International Gatherings of the Clans whenever they are held. Scottish heraldry takes a rather more liberal view regarding women, who are frequently recognized as Clan Chieftains and Lairds. This tends towards the assumption by male heirs of their mothers' surname and arms when familial succession has to pass through the female line.

Grants of titles of nobility on the Continent differ greatly from the system adopted in Britain. In France families able to trace their descent to 1400 or earlier were entitled to consider themselves the equal, or peers, of the King, and were known as feudal families. Quasi-feudal families were those able to prove an uninterrupted descent coupled with the possession of a fief from before 1560, and were called gentlemen of rank, birth or blood and could assume titles at will. In England the lowest rank of the peerage is the baron, in France the écuyer or esquire. The term 'Seigneur' is the equivalent of the English Lord of the Manor, and no matter whether you were a seigneur or a duc, you owed your nobility (noblesse) to the fact that you were an écuyer. Whether you called yourself Baron, Vicomte, Comte, Marquis or Duc depended upon the number of seigneuries you owned. Thus nobility and titles depended upon the size of your property, not, as in England, on a grant by the sovereign. It was the land or 'terre' which was deemed to be a Baronie, Comté or Marquisat, not the individual who possessed it. It did not follow that the son of a Marquis was a Comte or the son of a Comte a Vicomte as in England, where an individual or family rises through the ranks of the peerage so that a member of the family of A could be ennobled as Baron B, and later becomes Viscount C, Earl of D and Duke of E. In noble English families, subsidiary titles are used by courtesy only, e.g. the Duke of Grafton whose subsidiary titles, which may be borne by his eldest son and grandson until he inherits the dukedom, are Earl of Euston, Viscount Ipswich, and Baron Sudbury.

The use of heraldic arms in France has never been as strictly controlled as it has been in England and there is no French equivalent of the College of Arms. Arms, therefore, were not the privilege of noblemen. In 1696 Louis XIV instituted a General Armorial of France to register all coats of arms of gentlemen as well as those of ecclesiastics, burgesses and of those who enjoyed certain privileges and public rights.

In Austria and Germany since the sixteenth century the

nobility has been divided into Fürsten (princes), Grafen (counts) and Freiherren (barons) which together comprise the landed class of the high nobility. The emperors tended to honour more and more families with hereditary titles to the extent that it is possible to talk of a kind of 'inflation' of titles. Much the same situation obtained in Italy, where the proliferation of small sovereign states within the Holy Roman Empire gave rise to a plethora of titled families. In Spain the titles of Vizconde, Conde, Marqués and Duque were first granted in the fourteenth century and made hereditary through primogeniture and by right of succession as in Britain. These titles, although personal, were founded either on domains that already had titles attached to them or on new lands granted by the sovereign. The right to bear arms was restricted in Navarre to the nobility. In 1595 Kings of Arms were introduced by Philip II with powers not unlike those enjoyed by their English and Scottish counterparts. The powers of this body were confirmed by law in 1951 so that arms may still be granted in Spain today much in the same way as they are in Britain.

CHAPTER FOURTEEN
Maps

Those who are fortunate enough to find that their ancestors lived in the same town or village for generations are comparatively few. In 1973, Dr Peter Spufford, in a paper given before the Society of Genealogists, quoted from Professor Chamber's findings from the Vale of Trent, that nearly half the people died in different parishes from those in which they were born, but that a very large proportion of them, including many who died in the same parish in which they were born, lived for many years in yet other parishes. He was referring to seventeenth and eighteenth century studies. Other demographers have shown that apart from the great flow of people to London, practically all movement was restricted to a very limited distance, less than twenty miles, and a great deal of it less than ten miles. Studies in France, Italy and Hungary amongst societies of very different structure, have shown similar movements of population from as early as the fifteenth century. Of course the Industrial Revolution increased migration of this kind, especially in England, where it began earlier and continued longer.

This movement, coupled with the loss of records or their inability to show where people came from, causes many family historians to give up their research. It is at this point that real detective work is needed, and every piece of evidence must be used. Among the most useful tools at this stage are maps.

The factors inducing people to move are many, so a detailed study of local history, especially with regard to the growth of industries and the increase in enclosures, coupled with the study of local maps is now vital. County archivists are usually equipped to help you find out the history of the neighbourhood in which you are interested.

The earliest maps are those printed in the fifteenth century, but not many of these survive. Christopher Saxton's are among the earliest, followed in the seventeenth century by John Speed's maps of England and Robert Morden's in the eighteenth.

Estate maps which date from about 1570 and continue to 1860 are very useful in showing the layout of towns and villages at any given time. A series of such maps can show the progress of urban growth that accompanied the changes to many towns and villages during the Industrial Revolution.

The Enclosure Awards record the terms of enclosure and the disposition of all affected common land. An Award may be accompanied by a map which surveyors drew up to show how the common land was divided, and in some cases the whole village was shown in order to delineate the property in relation to the enclosure allotment that had been claimed. Medieval enclosures of open fields, moorland and meadow have often been agreed between the Lord of the Manor and other interested parties, but there were just as many enclosures made by stealth or even by brute force. In the sixteenth and early seventeenth centuries, the Courts of Exchequer and Chancery supervised enclosures, but after 1750 they were secured by Acts of Parliament. Since 1801 general Enclosure Acts have been made to facilitate enclosures.

The Anglo-Saxon tithes of one-tenth of the produce of land, stock or industry claimed by the church were a burden that led to disputes with farmers and landowners. The campaign to get them commuted into money payments finally resulted in the Tithe Commutation Act of 1836, and village meetings agreed on the value of tithes based on the average corn prices for the past seven years, and commissioners were appointed to award fair rents to be shared by all proprietors of land. Large-scale maps were drawn up by surveyors to show every parcel of land, path, garden, shed, outhouse, stream and factory, and apportionments set out in columns the names of owners and occupiers; description of each parcel of land; the state of cultivation and its acreage; and the tithe rent-charge. The Award, Map and Apportionment were fastened together and sealed. Three copies were produced, one for the Parish Chest, one for the Diocesan Registry, and one for the Land Registry. In 1936 rent charges were abolished, a stock fund was created to provide compensation, and all payments were planned to terminate in 1996.

Finally, there are the Ordnance Survey maps. These are probably the most frequently used by family historians. It is of course useful to have a copy of the current series for the area in which you are interested in order to locate places as they are today, but it is the first series of these maps that show what nineteenth-century Britain looked like. This edition is the one of greatest use in establishing the whereabouts of addresses obtained from census returns and civil registration certificates.

The Ordnance Survey, or Trigonometrical Survey as it was first named, was founded in 1791, its prime object being to produce a map of Great Britain to a scale of 1″ to the mile.

The first Ordnance Map, the 1″ to the mile map of Kent, was in fact privately published by William Faden, but the first official Old Series maps consisted of 110 sheets, mainly 36″ x 24″. This series was published between 1805 and 1873. These maps covered England and Wales, and, in terms of accuracy, are the least reliable. They should therefore be used critically. The New Series, or Second Edition, was started in 1840. There appears to have been a full-scale revision between 1893 and 1898, but all 360 sheets (12″ x 18″) were published before 1899. The survey for the Third Edition began in 1901, with publication between 1903 and 1913, again comprising 360 sheets, 12″ x 18″. The survey for the Fourth Edition started in 1913 and was published between 1918 and 1926. This marked a departure from its predecessors as it consisted of 146 sheets, 18″ x 27″. Various revised Editions have been published since the Fourth Edition, but for the purposes of research it is only the latest series that have any obvious relevance.

Although the 1″ to the mile maps formed the original series, larger scale maps of 6″ and 25″ to the mile were introduced during the second half of the nineteenth century to cover the whole of Britain. The 6″ survey was started in 1840, and the 25″ in 1853. In spite of considerable controversy, both from vested interests, private surveyors and on the grounds of economy, it was decided to make the 25″ series for the whole country, except for the uncultivated districts which were to be surveyed on the 6″ scale. From the 25″ maps, 6″ maps were produced by reduction. The First Edition of this series was completed between 1888 and 1893, the 25″ maps being on sheets 38″ x 25⅓″. The 6″ maps published before 1881 were on sheets 36″ x 24″, but thereafter they appeared in quarter sheets 18″ x 12″. The first revision began in 1891 and was completed in 1914. The second revision survey began in 1904, but was drastically interrupted by the First World War.

For this reason some areas were only partly revised, others not started, and the old system of revision was abandoned in 1922. Thereafter revision was confined to the 6″ sheets, and in 1928 this was replaced by continuous revision for areas of most rapid change. As with the 1″ series, these scales are available in the latest series.

It will be readily appreciated that the 1″ maps are most useful for research in a fairly large area, but once the exact place of interest has been located, it is essential to use the 6″ and 25″ maps for the very detailed information they can provide. The choice between the two larger scales will to a great extent depend on whether the area is urban or rural.

In addition to the main series of Ordnance Survey maps there are Town Plans found in a variety of scales and starting at different times; the first, for St Helens, was published in 1843. The usual and current sizes are those of 50″ to one mile, but all are worth examining for their superb workmanship and extensive detail. In some cases, even the number of seats within churches is shown.

There are of course other scales, in particular the 2½″ series, but for research purposes the above will invariably be sufficient.

Gazetteers are an essential accompaniment to maps. For the nineteenth century, the best is *Lewis's Topographical Dictionary*, which is divided into volumes covering England, Wales, Scotland and Ireland, each giving excellent details down to villages, hamlets and tithings. More recent publications are the Ordnance Survey and Bartholomew's Gazetteers which are adequate for use with current maps.

The British Library Map Library has one of the world's major historical collections of maps, charts, plans and topographical views, and also contains a comprehensive collection of modern maps of all countries. Similarly the copyright libraries – the National Library of Scotland, the National Library of Wales, the Bodleian Library at Oxford, Cambridge University Library and Trinity College Library, Dublin – hold extensive collections of maps, charts and plans. Indeed the best collection of Irish maps is at the library of Trinity College, Dublin. The Public Record Offices in London, Edinburgh, Belfast and Dublin, as well as the Royal Geographical Society, have their own unique and priceless collections.

County Record Offices have excellent collections for their

own areas, including Ordnance Survey maps. In addition there are the county reference libraries, museums, and specialist societies. All these valuable and helpful sources can often be used in conjunction with other research, or specific lines of enquiry.

The Institute of Heraldic and Genealogical Studies, Canterbury, has published a very useful series of parish maps for each county of England and Wales. Each map shows the ancient parochial boundaries, the Probate Court jurisdiction affecting each area in colour, and the dates of commencement of the original registers of each parish to have survived. These maps can be obtained separately from the Institute, or bound in book form, from the publishers, Everton Publishers Incorporated, Logan, Utah, USA.

For those interested in colonial America, several seventeenth- and eighteenth-century maps are available, but if you wish to study or plot the boundaries of original holdings in, for example, Virginia, then the most useful are the 7.5 minute series (topographic), published by the US Department of the Interior Geological Survey. In British terms, the scale is slightly over 2½" to the mile.

If your line of research peters out in a particular place, and further documentary evidence is not available to indicate where you should search next, you will have to examine the records of neighbouring parishes in an ever-increasing circle for the next clue or link, to enable you to find the evidence you are seeking. As Gerald Hamilton-Edwards has pointed out: 'Villagers would often walk up the road in search of refreshment and change, and many a village lad met his future bride through first contacting her father or brother in the neighbouring "local".' With the higher classes this may well be the neighbouring county, but as these people are usually better documented, the problem does not so often arise until one gets back to the sixteenth century or earlier.

MAPS

The counties of England, Wales and Scotland before and after boundary reorganization.

THE COUNTIES OF ENGLAND

1 BEDFORDSHIRE
2 BERKSHIRE
3 BUCKINGHAMSHIRE
4 CAMBRIDGESHIRE AND ISLE OF ELY
5 CHESHIRE
6 CORNWALL
7 CUMBERLAND
8 DERBYSHIRE
9 DEVON
10 DORSET
11 COUNTY DURHAM
12 ESSEX
13 GLOUCESTERSHIRE
14 GREATER LONDON
15 HAMPSHIRE
16 HEREFORDSHIRE
17 HERTFORDSHIRE
18 HUNTINGDON AND PETERBOROUGH
19 KENT
20 LANCASHIRE
21 LEICESTERSHIRE
22 LINCOLNSHIRE (HOLLAND; KESTEVEN, AND LINDSEY)
23 MONMOUTHSHIRE
24 NORFOLK
25 NORTHAMPTONSHIRE
26 NORTHUMBERLAND
27 NOTTINGHAMSHIRE
28 OXFORDSHIRE
29 RUTLAND
30 SHROPSHIRE
31 SOMERSET
32 STAFFORDSHIRE
33 SUFFOLK (EAST AND WEST)
34 SURREY
35 SUSSEX (EAST AND WEST)
36 WARWICKSHIRE
37 WESTMORLAND
38 WILTSHIRE
39 WORCESTERSHIRE
40 YORKSHIRE (EAST, NORTH, AND WEST RIDINGS)

THE COUNTIES OF WALES

41 ANGLESEY
42 BRECKNOCK
43 CAERNARVONSHIRE
44 CARDIGANSHIRE
45 CARMARTHENSHIRE
46 DENBIGHSHIRE
47 FLINTSHIRE
48 GLAMORGAN
49 MERIONETH
50 MONTGOMERYSHIRE
51 PEMBROKESHIRE
52 RADNOR

THE COUNTIES OF SCOTLAND

53 ABERDEENSHIRE
54 ANGUS
55 ARGYLL
56 AYRSHIRE
57 BANFFSHIRE
58 BERWICKSHIRE
59 BUTE
60 CAITHNESS
61 CLACKMANNANSHIRE
62 DUMFRIESSHIRE
63 DUNBARTONSHIRE
64 EAST LOTHIAN
65 FIFE
66 INVERNESS-SHIRE
67 KINCARDINESHIRE
68 KINROSS-SHIRE
69 KIRKCUDBRIGHTSHIRE
70 LANARKSHIRE
71 MIDLOTHIAN
72 MORAY
73 NAIRNSHIRE
74 ORKNEY ISLANDS
75 PEEBLESSHIRE
76 PERTHSHIRE
77 RENFREWSHIRE
78 ROSS AND CROMARTY
79 ROXBURGHSHIRE
80 SELKIRKSHIRE
81 SHETLAND ISLANDS
82 STIRLINGSHIRE
83 SUTHERLAND
84 WEST LOTHIAN
85 WIGTOWNSHIRE

MAPS

THE COUNTIES OF ENGLAND

1 AVON
2 BEDFORDSHIRE
3 BERKSHIRE
4 BUCKINGHAMSHIRE
5 CAMBRIDGESHIRE
6 CHESHIRE
7 CLEVELAND
8 CORNWALL
9 CUMBRIA
10 DERBYSHIRE
11 DEVON
12 DORSET
13 DURHAM
14 EAST SUSSEX
15 ESSEX
16 GLOUCESTERSHIRE
17 GREATER LONDON
18 GREATER MANCHESTER
19 HAMPSHIRE
20 HEREFORD AND WORCESTER
21 HERTFORDSHIRE
22 HUMBERSIDE
23 ISLE OF WIGHT
24 KENT
25 LANCASHIRE
26 LEICESTERSHIRE
27 LINCOLNSHIRE
28 MERSEYSIDE
29 NORFOLK
30 NORTHAMPTONSHIRE
31 NORTHUMBERLAND
32 NORTH YORKSHIRE
33 NOTTINGHAMSHIRE
34 OXFORDSHIRE
35 SALOP
36 SOMERSET
37 SOUTH YORKSHIRE
38 STAFFORDSHIRE
39 SUFFOLK
40 SURREY
41 TYNE AND WEAR
42 WARWICKSHIRE
43 WEST MIDLANDS
44 WEST SUSSEX
45 WEST YORKSHIRE
46 WILTSHIRE

THE COUNTIES OF WALES

47 CLWYD
48 DYFED
49 GWENT
50 GWYNEDD
51 MID GLAMORGAN
52 POWYS
53 SOUTH GLAMORGAN
54 WEST GLAMORGAN

THE COUNTIES OF SCOTLAND

55 BORDERS REGION
56 CENTRAL REGION
57 DUMFRIES AND GALLOWAY REGION
58 FIFE REGION
59 GRAMPIAN REGION
60 HIGHLAND REGION
61 LOTHIAN REGION
62 ORKNEY ISLANDS AREA
63 SHETLAND ISLANDS AREA
64 STRATHCLYDE REGION
65 TAYSIDE REGION
66 WESTERN ISLES ISLAND AREA

137

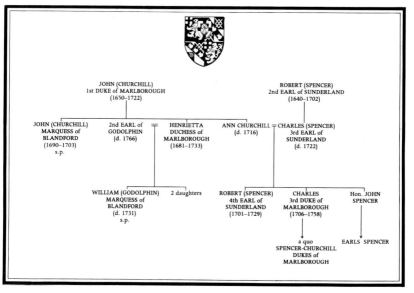

The extract from a family tree shows how the surname Spencer-Churchill arose. Charles Spencer, 3rd Earl of Sunderland married the younger daughter of John Churchill, 1st Duke of Marlborough. Following the death of her elder sister without surviving male heirs, the dukedom together with the names Spencer and Churchill came to the second son of the Earl of Sunderland. The earl's youngest son continues to use the name Spencer only and was the father of the 1st Earl Spencer.

The arms shown are those of Spencer and Churchill quartered together.

City or Borough of _____

Parish or Township of _East Peckham_

Enumeration Schedule.

PLACE	HOUSES Uninhabited or Building	HOUSES Inhabited	NAMES of each Person who abode therein the preceding Night.	AGE and SEX Males	AGE and SEX Females	PROFESSION, TRADE, EMPLOYMENT, or of INDEPENDENT MEANS.	Whether Born in same County	Whether Born in Scotland, Ireland, or Foreign Parts
			John Grayland		15	F S	yes	
Fox's House		1	Thomas Martin	35		Farmer	yes	
			Maria do		30		no	
			Edwin do	5			no	
			Emily do		2		do	
			Frederick do	1 month			do	
			Ann Batchelor		20	F S	do	
			Caroline Colegate		20	F S	do	
			Louisa Ecrall		20	F S	do	
			William Greenaway	25		M S	do	
			Henry Jupp	12		M S	do	
Mount Pleasant		1	Martha Andrews		60	Independent	yes	
			William Dunk	62		M S	do	
			Caroline Wilson		25	F S	do	
			Bethany Freeman		19	F S	do	
near the Court Lodge		1	George Scott	29		Ag Lab	yes	
			Mary do		21		do	
			Mary do		3		do	
			Elizabeth do		2		do	
			Harriott do		2 month		do	
			Sarah Underdown		11		do	
do		1	George Bishop	28		Ag Lab	yes	
			Harriott do		30		do	
			Robert do	8			do	
			John do	5			do	
TOTAL in Page 8	4			10	15			

B c

3 f 9

Parish or Township of	Ecclesiastical District of	City or Borough of	Town of	Village of

No. of House	Name of Street, Place, or Road, and Name or No. of House	Name and Surname of each Person who abode in the house, on the Night of the 30th March, 1851	Relation to Head of Family	Condition	Age of Male	Age of Female	Rank, Profession, or Occupation	Where Born	Whether Blind, or Deaf-and-Dumb
68	Hextle House (Cottage)	Richard Street	Servant	Unm	21		Farmer Servant	Kent East Peckham	
		William Jupp	Head	Mar	32		Gardener	Kent East Peckham	
		Mary Jupp	Wife	Mar		42		Kent Penshurst	
		Matilda Jupp	Daur			9	Scholar	Kent East Peckham	
69	Pond Farm	Robert Lipscomb	Head	Mar	84		Farmer of 130 acres employing 8 labourers	Kent Tonbridge	
		Elizabeth Lipscomb	Wife	Mar		56	Farmer's Wife	Kent Spaldhurst	
		Martha Lipscomb	Daur	Unm		19	Farmer's Daughter	Kent Penshurst	
		Anne Oxley	Relation	Unm		28		Kent Penshurst	
70	Hextle House	Maria Martin	Head	Mar		42	Landed Proprietor	Sussex Hove	
		Anna Martin	Daur	Unm		9		Kent East Peckham	
		Leslie Martin	Son					Kent East Peckham	
		Caroline Bracknay	Sister	Unm		43		Sussex Hove	
		Helen Murdoch	Servant	Unm		19	Governess	Middlesex St Pancras	
		Fanny Saunders	Servant	Unm		20	House Servant	Kent East Peckham	
		Ann Oram	do	Unm		27	House Servant	Sussex Lamberhurst	
		Mary Rogers	do	Unm		25	House Servant	Kent East Peckham	
		George Burrows	do	Unm	21		Ag Lab	Kent Wrotham	

Total of Houses 3   Total of Persons 5 12

LEFT AND ABOVE

Comparison of these extracts from the census returns of 1841 (left)
and 1851 (above) for Hextle House, East Peckham, shows that
Thomas Martin died between the two dates and that his wife
Maria only gave her approximate age in the earlier census, as
required by the rules. In the 1851 return the precise place of birth
is given and the children Edwin and Emily appear to have died.
Leslie's birth, which took place during 1848 or 1849, gives an
indication of the approximate date of Thomas's death.

Abigal	wife of John Landsmore was buried June 4
Elizabeth	wife of Robert Plummer was buried July 30
Richard	Stevens an Infant was buried August 13
Tobillia	Major Infant buried Aug 30
John	Bradly was buried Sept. 14
Elizab:	wife of George Baker bur: Sep 18
Elizab:	wife of William Alderton was buried Sept. 21
Ruth	Carvel, buried. October 3
William	Brundwood buried Octo 9
Ruth	Cobbin, buried. October 13
Ann	Bradley buried October 13
Elizab:	wife of Abraham Landsell was buried October 15
Mary	Goldsmith an Infant was buried November 1st
Wm	Doe Infant buried Nov 28
Robt	Arthur, buried Jan: 23
George	Dale buried Feb 9th

William Pawlett Curate
Abra: Wetherell }
Robt Butler } Church

Anno Dñi 1722

Elizab:	Swan Wid buried April 7
John	Bumpstead an Infant was buried April 21
John	Norman an Infant was buried May 1st
John	Merriol was buried July 16
John	Nichols was buried July 19
William	Lunt, an Infant was buried July 26
Maynard	Doe a base begotten child was buried August 18
John	Robinson buried Jan: 26

Abra	Landsell buried October 4
Dinah	Bennett an Infant bur Octo 28
Frances	Goldsmith buried October 29
Margt	Landsell an Infant buried Nov 8
John	Waller Gibson Infant buried February 14
Stephen	Row, Infant, buried Feb: 17
Alice	Hammond an Infant was buried February 21

Chr: Grove Curate
Abraham Wetherell }
Robert Butler } Church

1723

Sarah	Goldsmith buried May 28
Mary	Randell was buried June 26
Sarah	Smith was buried July 19
Bridget	Dexter of Stanton was buried August 17
Ann	Parker Infant bur Augt 23
Charles	Medcalfe buried Sept. 20
Susan	Landsmore buried Sept 22
Barbara	the wife of Samuel Alderton was buried October 5
Margt	Ireland buried November 4
John	Gaugitt an Infant buried Nov 16
John	Clarke buried November 22
John	Bennit an Infant was buried January 12
Ann	Norman buried Jan: 30
Wm	Crick an Infant was buried March 6
Wm	Chambers was buried March 9
Elizab:	Crack an Infant buried March 17
Richd	Bennitt an Infant was buried March 25

Chr: Grove Curate
Abra: Wetherell }
Robt Butler } Church

Sampson Lloyd of Birmingham in the County of Warwick Ironmonger and Sarah Parks Daughter of Richard Parks of Birmingham aforesaid Ironmonger Having declared their Intentions of taking each other in Marriage before several Publick Meetings of the People of God called Quakers in Warwickshire according to the Good Order used among them whose Proceedings therein after a deliberate Consideration thereof (with regard unto the Righteous Law of God and Example of his People Recorded in the Scriptures of Truth in that Case) were approved by the said Meetings they appearing clear of all others and having Consent of Parents and Relations concerned

Now these are to certifie all whom it may concern That for the full accomplishing of their said Intentions this Twenty Ninth Day of the Ninth Month called November in the Year according to the English Account One Thousand Seven Hundred and Twenty Seven They the said Sampson Lloyd and Sarah Parks appeared in a Publick Assembly of the aforesaid People and others met together for that end and purpose in their Publick Meeting Place at Birmingham aforesaid and in a solemn Manner he the said Sampson Lloyd taking the said Sarah Parks by the Hand did openly declare as followeth Friends in the Presence of God and this Assembly I take this my Friend Sarah Parks to be my Wife promising with Gods Assistance to be unto Her a loving and faithfull Husband till Death shall seperate us And then and there in the said Assembly the said Sarah Parks did in like manner declare as followeth Friends in the Presence of God and this Assembly I take this my Friend Sampson Lloyd to be my Husband promising with Gods Assistance to be unto him a loving and faithfull Wife till Death shall seperate us and the said Sampson Lloyd and Sarah Parks as a further Confirmation thereof did then and there to these Presents set their Hands and we whose Names are hereunto subscribed being present among others at the Solemnizing of their said Marriage and Subscription in manner afforesaid as Witnesses hereunto have also to these Presents Subscribed our Names the Day and Year above written

This Quaker marriage certificate of 1727 gives more information than is found on Church of England marriage entries of the same date. Note that the names of the witnesses, many of whom could be related to the bride or groom, are given.

A typical eighteenth-century country parish register from Ickworth, Suffolk showing burials for part of the period 1721-1723. Later in the century special printed registers were produced in which particulars were recorded uniformly throughout England and Wales.

and my bodie to be buried in the parish Church yarde of ... ...
... ... item I give unto Lawrence Stump my youngest sonne ten pounds item
I give unto William Stump my ... sonne one pound and his lambe item I give unto
James Stump my sonne two pounds and one ... and his lambe item I give unto
Marie James daughter to William James one ... shillings item I give to the poore
and to ... in the Collection every yeare of them one peck of wheate and Rye
the rest of my goods not disposed of my debts being paid my funerall expences discharged
I make mine ordeyne ... my wife ... and Lawrence my sonne full Executors of
this my last will and testament in ... witnesses John Burnham Wilford Cooke
James Crump his marke

The second Day of November in the year of our Lord God one thousand
six hundred sixty upper there issued forth letters of Administration unto Lawrence
Stump the grandfather of James and Lawrence Stump minors the sonne and
... executors named in the will of the sayd deceased according to the tenor and
effect of the sayd will during the minoritie and to the use of the sayd Minors and being
by vertue of a Commission in that behalfe ... forth first sworne truly to Administer
the same

the first day of
March in the yeare of our lord God according to the computation of the Church of England
one thousand six hundreth sixtie and two I ... ... of Kilmerton in ...
in the County of ... yeoman being of sound and perfect memory and understanding
... and considering any ... ... the sayety and instability of this ... this
life do make and ordeyne this my last will and testament in manner and forme following
that is to say first and principally I Commend my soule into the hands of Almighty god
my maker and redeemer trusting in and through the merites of our lord and saviour Jesus
Christ to be one of that blessed Company to whome there is full sentence ... of
blessed of my father receive the Kingdome prepared for you ... And
my bodie I commend to Christian buriall at her discretion of my ... to be buried ...
... con... And as touching and disposition of my temporall estate which god of his good ...
... lent unto me ... the avoiding of all difference that might after my death ... arise
about the same ... will and mynde is as followeth first where as I have already given and
... upon Henry Curver and John Curver my two younger sonnes the summe of ...
hundreth pounds apeece in liew ... and full satisfaction of their childs partes and
portions as appeareth by a generall release under my hande bearing date the first day of
October one thousand six hundred forty and eight 1648 I ... give ...
... of them one hundred pounds of Current English money to better and further ...
... childs parte and portions ... ... given of both of them two hundred ...
pounds owing to me by Hugh Curver my sonne and ... apparent unto Mary Curver
my daughter in liew or the childs parte and portion for which sayd ... Hugh Curver
hath sealed and ... me two ... will condition ... obligatory for the payment ... of
accordingly ... as I have already given and bestowed upon ... Item in more ...
daughter the summe of two hundred and ... pound in ... ... and full satisfaction of her childs parte and portion as by a ... release ... ... Day of January
in the yeare of our Lord God one thousand six hundred ... ... sealed and delivered
unto me by William Watson me name and more fully appeareth And where as I
have likewise given and bestowed upon Martha ... my daughter the summe
of five hundred pounds sterling in liew and full satisfaction of her childs part
and portion as may ... ... release sealed and delivered pursuant by Edmund Baldwin
his his bond bearing date the eight day of July in the yeare of our Lord God one thousand
six hundred and fifty more fully may appeare Now that is for my will and mynde is
that all my debts and ... due at my death be paid and discharged out of my whole
personall estate And after payment thereof my will and mynde is And I ... do hereby give
and bequeath unto the aforenamed Mary my ... the summe of five ...
hundred

ABOVE

The deposition of a witness in a case brought before the Chancery
Court on 4 May 1627. Lionel Rolston describes how he was living
in Virginia and how, before he went, he received certain annuities
from his friends. He gives his age as 37. (Class C.24).

OPPOSITE

The Will of Henry Currer of Kildwick, Yorkshire, 1652. This is part
of the register copy in the Prerogative Court of Canterbury.

An eighteenth-century land-purchase bond in which William
Trefusis Reichenberg of Devereux Court, St Clement Danes,
London, and John Rodolphus Reichenberg of St Buryan, Cornwall,
are bound to Elizabeth Trefusis to pay her £600.
The penalty for failure to pay is £1200.

CHAPTER FIFTEEN
The Professional Approach

It has to be admitted at the outset that genealogy is a hobby, and that those who undertake to trace their ancestors want to do it for themselves. It is, however, equally true that often this is impossible. If you trace your ancestry to some part of the country remote from that in which you live, or if you are an American or Australian wanting to trace the origin of your emigrant ancestors, it becomes necessary sometimes to seek professional help. Amateur researchers often know a great deal about their own families, but they cannot be expected to know exactly what steps they should take to further their research. The professional genealogist, therefore, exists mainly to help those who have 'got stuck'. For over 200 years, Debrett have chronicled the families of the aristocracy. Debrett Ancestry Research Ltd now researches families from all walks of life in Britain, Ireland North America and Australasia.

Amateurs tend to place too literal a trust in documents and what they say. There is a reluctance to accept variations in the spelling of a surname, forgetting that the document they are reading was written not by the person they're looking for, but by a clerk who wrote down phonetically what he heard. A fine example of this is the indentured servant who turned up in Bristol *en route* for America in the 1660s, and when asked by the clerk where he came from replied with a name the clerk recorded as 'Sneeds'. Another was recorded as coming from 'Nutcheter'. Of course neither of these places exist, but the town of St Neots in Huntingdonshire is pronounced 'Saint Neets' and the town of Uttoxeter in Staffordshire used to be pronounced 'Utcheter'. A professional will be used to coping with this kind of problem. Then there is the problem of dates before 1752 (see page 77), and the falsification of ages. Men joined the services while still under age, and often married without their parents' consent, and consequently gave a wrong age to the clerk.

The Association of Genealogists and Record Agents (AGRA) was founded in 1968 in order to promote and maintain high standards among all professional practitioners, and to protect the interests of both members and clients. Clients can receive a list of reliable genealogists and record agents with details of their interests and specialities by sending £1.50 (UK, 1992 price) or five international reply coupons (overseas) to the Secretary, 29 Badgers Close, Horsham, West Sussex RH12 5RU. Only well-qualified and experienced persons who have been engaged as professional genealogists and/or record agents for a number of years are eligible for membership.

In general terms, the genealogist directs the research, whereas the record agent undertakes it. The genealogist, therefore, acts as a consultant, setting the line of enquiry and initiating, supervising and participating in the work that it entails. He or she will then report to the client and suggest possible lines of further research as appropriate. The work of the record agent lies in searching specified records for particular information which may be required by a genealogist, historian, biographer or amateur client. However, many members of AGRA act in both capacities as the need arises.

The association does not undertake any research work itself. If you wish to employ a genealogist or record agent you should select a suitable one from the list of members, having regard to the part of the country in which the research will need to be carried out. Having selected someone appropriate, you should then send a preliminary letter setting out the problem, and stating clearly the relevant and known facts, enclosing a stamped, addressed envelope (if you live in the UK) or three international reply coupons (if you live abroad).

With regard to cost, it is always very difficult to estimate this in advance. Members' fees are based on an hourly rate for the time spent (including the giving of advice), to which must be added the cost of disbursements (photocopies, church and government fees, travel time and so on). Most researchers will be prepared to give an estimate for searching within a limited number of specified records, but in more open-ended cases he or they will probably ask you to set a limit upon the amount of money you wish to spend in the first instance (e.g. £50, £100, £500). In such cases it is customary for all (or part of the fee in cases of £100 and over) of the fee to be paid in advance, and when the researcher has exhausted this amount the results of the enquiries will be fully reported, with details of any problems met with, and further avenues of research will be suggested for you to consider. It is then up to you to decide whether or not you wish to embark on any further research.

Once a genealogist or record agent has agreed to carry out research, it is most important for them to have all relevant information, distinguishing between what is certain and proveable and what is only traditional, thus ensuring that they do not have to spend time establishing facts you knew already.

Members of AGRA, apart from having proved their professional competence upon application, agree to comply with a detailed code of practice, which stresses the need for a high standard of work as well as complete confidentiality. Copies of this code of practice can be obtained from the secretary of AGRA on receipt of a stamped addressed envelope or two international reply coupons.

Appendix I: Table of Regnal Years

Many official documents and wills refer to dates in terms of the year of the reign of the sovereign in question, e.g. 26 June 13 Chas II (26 June 1661). The regnal year dates from the first day of the reign of each sovereign, thus the first year of Queen Elizabeth I began on 17 November 1558, the date of her accession, and lasted until 16 November 1559.

The following is a list of the regnal years of the kings and queens since the Norman Conquest.

William I 14 Oct 1066 to 9 Sep 1087
William II 9 Sep 1087 to 1 Aug 1100
Henry I 1 Aug 1100 to 2 Dec 1135
Stephen 2 Dec 1135 to 25 Oct 1154
Henry II 25 Oct 1154 to 13 Aug 1189
Richard I 13 Aug 1189 to 6 Apr 1199
John 6 Apr 1199 to 17 Oct 1216
Henry III 17 Oct 1216 to 16 Nov 1272
Edward I 16 Nov 1272 to 8 Jul 1307
Edward II 8 Jul 1307 to 25 Jan 1326/7
Edward III 25 Jan 1326/7 to 22 Jun 1377
Richard II 22 Jun 1377 to 30 Sep 1399
Henry IV 30 Sep 1399 to 21 Mar 1412/13
Henry V 21 Mar 1412/13 to 1 Sep 1422
Henry VI 1 Sep 1422 to 4 Mar 1460/1
Edward IV 4 Mar 1460/1 to 9 Apr 1483
Edward V 9 Apr 1483 to 22 Jun 1483
Richard III 22 Jun 1483 to 22 Aug 1485
Henry VII 22 Aug 1485 to 22 Apr 1509
Henry VIII 22 Apr 1509 to 28 Jan 1546/7
Edward VI 28 Jan 1546/7 to 6 Jul 1553
Mary I and Philip 6 Jul 1553 to 17 Nov 1558
Elizabeth I 17 Nov 1558 to 24 Mar 1602/3
James I 24 Mar 1602/3 to 27 Mar 1625/6
Charles I 27 Mar 1625/6 to 30 Jan 1648/9

(*Note* The assumption is that there is a complete continuity of the Crown, and therefore the throne is never vacant. Despite the interregnum, Charles II ascended the throne upon the death of Charles I and remained in exile until 1660. Dates during the interregnum are usually given in *anno Domini*.)

Charles II 30 Jan 1648/9 to 6 Feb 1684/5
James II 6 Feb 1684/5 to 13 Feb 1688/9
William III and Mary II 13 Feb 1688/9 to 28 Dec 1694
William III alone 13 Feb 1694/5 to 8 Mar 1701/2
Anne 8 Mar 1701/2 to 1 Aug 1714
George I 1 Aug 1714 to 11 Jun 1727
George II 11 Jun 1727 to 25 Oct 1760
George III 25 Oct 1760 to 29 Jan 1820
George IV 29 Jan 1820 to 26 Jun 1830
William IV 26 Jun 1830 to 20 Jun 1837
Victoria 20 Jun 1837 to 22 Jan 1901

From the beginning of the reign of Queen Victoria, a knowledge of the regnal years is not of any importance for genealogical purposes, since all documents were dated *anno Domini*.

Appendix II: The Generation Grid and its Uses

Anyone who has attempted to compile a family history will have come up against the problem of how to distinguish between several individuals of the same forename and surname living at approximately the same period of time. Before the middle of the eighteenth century, to have more than one given name (in Britain, at any rate) was rare, and the confusion arising from this has led many a researcher to make some seriously mistaken identifications. Nowhere is this more true than in the field of Anglo-colonial pedigrees, where the incorrect identification of an emigrant has resulted in some totally false claims and descents.

One way to overcome this confusion is the use of the generation grid where a standard series of identifying letters is allotted to the generations.

A = 1380–1409		L = 1710–1739	
B = 1410–1439		M = 1740–1769	
C = 1440–1469		N = 1770–1799	
D = 1470–1499		O = 1800–1829	
E = 1500–1529		P = 1830–1859	
F = 1530–1559		Q = 1860–1889	
G = 1560–1589		R = 1890–1919	
H = 1590–1619		S = 1920–1949	
I = 1620–1649		T = 1950–1979	
J = 1650–1679		U = 1980–2009	
K = 1680–1709			

We next make a list of the given names in each generation (and for the sake of brevity the following is confined to the names of males only). Let us suppose that in generation 'K' of a family there are four Williams, three Christophers, two Henrys, two Edwards, one each of Hugh, Walter, Anthony, Gregory and John; and in generation 'L' six Williams, four Hughs, three Johns, two Henrys, two Walters, two Thomases, one each of Christopher, Samuel, Arthur, Peter, Gregory and Richard.

The number of female names can similarly be listed. It should be possible from the scraps of pedigree and from isolated and untabulated information gathered during the search to establish the exact or approximate year of birth of each individual. Having established the broad outlines of each generation, everyone born between 1680 and 1709 will be allocated the letter K followed by two digits, thus: K01-49 for men and K50-99 for women. Let us suppose that the six children of, for example, Hugh Kildwick (K02) (born 1705) are William, Christopher, Peter, Francis, Isabel and Anne, all born between 1726 and 1735. These will be allocated references in generation L thus: L01, L02, L03, L04, L50 and L51 respectively. Similarly the children of Hugh Kildwick (K08) (born 1695) whom we have found elsewhere to be Grace, Peter, Thomas, Francis, Matthew, Henry, Jeremy, Elizabeth, Joan and Margaret, all of whom were born between 1717 and 1730, are allocated the references L52, L05, L06, L07, L08, L09, L10, L53, L54 and L55. Thus Peter (L03) can be immediately distinguished from Peter (L05).

Anyone using the generation grid system knows by heart which generations the letters 'K' and 'L' cover, and would not have to keep referring to a key. Also, the generations in different pedigrees are immediately comparable, so that one can make a reasonable guess whether one person could be the son or daughter of another without doing complicated sums. Stray references to members of the family, whose place in the pedigree cannot immediately be established, are similarly allocated reference numbers within the generation to which they appear to belong. In cases of doubt – say, when the precise date of birth is not known, but where it could be within a span of years bridging two generations, e.g. between 1705 and 1715 – the letters KL would be used until such time as the precise date is discovered. The use of a generation grid in conjunction with the dates of different records as printed in Appendix III helps to establish the sources in which searches for any particular generation should best be made.

Appendix III: A Records Date List

It is important to be aware of certain dates when searching documents in which to look for information. The following is a list of some of those most useful to genealogists. The generation letter in the right-hand column refers to the generation grid as described in Appendix II.

1509	HENRY VIII	1500–29
1522	Earliest known Muster Roll	Generation E
1538	Parish registers ordered to be kept	1530–59
1542	Administrative Union of Wales with England	Generation F
1547	EDWARD VI	
1552	Ulster King of Arms established	
1553	MARY I	
1558	ELIZABETH I	
1558	Chancery Proceedings C.2 & C.3 Indexes begin	
1567	Earliest Huguenot & Walloon registers	1560–89
1574	Colonial State Papers published. Continued to 1738	Generation G
1578	Earliest Quaker registers	
1597	Bishops' Transcripts begin	1590–1619
1600	Memoirs of officers of the Royal Navy first kept	Generation H
1601	Poor Relief Act	
1601	East India Company founded	
1603	JAMES I and VI of Scotland	
1626	CHARLES I	1620–49
1642	Civil Wars interrupt parish register keeping	Generation I
1644	Earliest Presbyterian registers	
1644	Earliest Independent (Congregational) registers	
1645	Inquisitions *post mortem* end	
1647	Earliest Baptist registers	
1649	COMMONWEALTH	
1649	CHARLES II, but in exile	

1653	Provincial probate courts abolished	1650–79
1660	CHARLES II – the Restoration	Generation J
1660	Provincial probate courts re-established	
1660	Parish registers resumed	
1662	Poor Relief Act	
1662	Hearth Tax	
1663	Earliest Roman Catholic registers	
1667	Burial in woollen	
1669	Earliest Lutheran registers	
1670	Earliest Synagogue registers – Bevis Marks	
1677	Lee's Collection of Names of Merchants in London	
1679	Burial in woollen more strictly enforced	
1684	Huguenot registers begin in London	1680–1709
1685	JAMES II	Generation K
1688	Hearth Tax abolished	
1689	WILLIAM and MARY	
1689	Toleration Act for Protestant Nonconformists	
1689	Earliest Royal Dutch Chapel registers	
1690	Great Synagogue founded in London	
1695	Dissenters' lists of births in parish registers	
1698	Duties payable on entries in parish registers	
1702	ANNE	
1703	Repeat of duties on entries in parish registers	
1708	Earliest Artillery Muster Rolls	
1710	Tax on apprentice indentures	1710–39
1714	GEORGE I	Generation L
1714	Chancery proceedings filed under six clerks	
1721	Bailey's Northern Directory	
1727	GEORGE II	
1731	Abolition of Latin	
1732	Earliest Cavalry and Infantry Muster Rolls	
1734	Kent's Directory	
1738	Earliest Calvinistic Methodist registers	
1741	Earliest Moravian registers	1740–69
1741	Earliest Scotch Church registers	Generation M
1752	Gregorian Calendar introduced in Britain	

1752	Earliest Lady Huntingdon's New Connection registers	
1753	Earliest Inghamite registers	
1754	Lord Hardwicke's Marriage Act	
1754	First printed annual Army Lists	
1760	GEORGE III	
1762	Earliest Unitarian registers	
1762	Earliest Swiss Church registers	
1772	First Navy Lists	1770–99
1779	Earliest New Connection Methodist registers	Generation N
1780	Earliest Wesleyan registers	
1780	Male Servants Tax	
1783	Duty on parish register entries	
1784	New South Wales original correspondence C.O.201	
1787	Earliest Swedenborgian registers	
1790	Barfoot's London Commercial Directory	
1792	Boyle's Street Directory	
1794	Abolition of parish register duties	
1796	Holden's Triennial Directory	
1799	Post Office New Annual Directory	
1800	Royal College of Surgeons founded	1800–29
1800	Earliest Bible Christian registers	Generation O
1806	Earliest Primitive Methodist registers	
1813	Rose's Act—new parish register books	
1814	Act of burial in woollen repealed	
1814	Cape Colony C.O.48	
1814	Pigot's Commercial Directory	
1817	Johnstone's London Directory	
1820	GEORGE IV	
1823	New laws concerning marriage by licence	
1823	Scottish testaments prior to 1823 transferred to Scottish Records Office	
1826	White's first directory — Hull	
1829	Earliest Irvingite registers	
1830	WILLIAM IV	1830–59
1835	Earliest Universalist registers	Generation P
1837	VICTORIA	
1837	Civil registration in England and Wales	
1841	Census — first of value to genealogists	
1842	Civil registration in Channel Islands	

1845	Royal Naval Biographical Dictionary published	
1845	Kelly's Directories	
1845	Registration of Protestant marriages in Ireland	
1849	Civil registration of births Isle of Man	
1851	Census — of improved value to genealogists	
1855	Civil registration in Scotland	
1858	Central probate registry	
1861	Census	1860–89
1864	Civil registration in Ireland	Generation Q
1864	Civil registration of marriages Isle of Man	
1871	Census	
1872	Penalties for failing to register births, marriages and deaths	
1876	Civil registration of deaths Isle of Man	
1881	Census	
1891	Census	1890–1919
1901	EDWARD VII	Generation R
1901	Census	
	Open to public search after 2001	
1910	GEORGE V	
1916	Rebellion in Ireland	
1922	Partition of Ireland and destruction of Four Courts	1920–49
		Generation S
1927	Adoption registration—records kept at General Register Office	
1937	EDWARD VIII	
1937	GEORGE VI	
1943	Ulster King of Arms transferred to Dublin	
1952	ELIZABETH II	1950–79
1975	Children's Acts–amends previous Adoption Acts	Generation T

Appendix IV: A Checklist of Genealogical Sources

Group I—Private Records, Papers and Relics

1 Family Bible
2 Family pedigree or other written account, notes or memoranda by members of the family concerning its history and traditions
3 Diaries
4 Notebooks about family events
5 Birthday books
6 Account books
7 Stock, share and tontine (annuity) certificates
8 Deeds relating to property, including estate maps
9 Marriage contracts and settlements
10 Baptismal certificates and other records
11 Barmitzvah cards
12 Confirmation and first communion certificates
13 Funeral cards
14 Bank books, life assurance policies
15 School and university records, certificates and prizes
16 Degrees
17 Certificates of ordination
18 Driving and similar licences
19 Passports, identity cards, denizations, naturalizations
20 Testimonials
21 Sporting prizes and cups
22 Letters
23 Bookplates
24 Club and professional association membership records
25 Trade union records
26 Armed service records
27 Medals and decorations
28 Civic awards
29 Samplers
30 Mourning and signet rings, seals and fobs
31 Crested or armorial silver, glass and china
32 Portraits and photographs
33 Records of changes of name
34 Divorce proceedings and settlements
35 Medical certificates and records

Group II—Public Records

36 Wills
37 Marriage proclamations (banns) and licences
38 Marriage certificates and bonds
39 Birth certificates
40 Death certificates
41 Burial records, receipts for mort cloths, leasehold and freehold records of burial plots, cremation certificates, graveyard and cemetery records, monumental inscriptions
42 Apprenticeship indentures
43 East India Company records
44 Family lawyers' records
45 Hatchments, paintings and engravings or armorial bearings
46 Certificates of grants of arms
47 Records of lawsuits concerning intestacies and illegitimacies
48 Adoption records
49 Documents relating to criminal conviction and transportation
50 Patents for inventions
51 Grants and patents of land and feet of fines
52 Master mariners' certificates and the like
53 Notarial records
54 Census records
55 Parish registers
56 Bishops' and archdeacons' transcripts
57 Inquisitions *post mortem*
58 Royalist composition papers
59 Protestation returns and oaths of allegiance
60 Records of the court of law

Group III—Miscellaneous Records and Indexes

61 Obituaries
62 Names of houses, estates and plantations associated with the family
63 Local and national newspapers and journals; press cuttings
64 Biographies and autobiographies
65 Local and national directories
66 Publications – books, articles, poems, etc.
67 Genealogical guides and reference books
68 International Genealogical Index (IGI) (Mormon Genealogical Collections)
69 National Pedigree Index (Society of Genealogists)
70 Directories of members' interests published by UK family history and genealogical societies
71 Collections of deposited pedigrees at Society of Genealogists, county record offices, libraries, etc.

72　Catalogue of British Library printed books (reference to family histories or biographies) and MS collections
73　Topographical dictionaries
74　Titles of unpublished theses submitted to British universities
75　Records of Houses of Parliament
76　Ordnance Survey, tithe and enclosure maps
77　The Return of Owners of Land 1873 ('Modern Domesday Book')

Appendix V: Record Offices, Libraries and Societies

Before carrying out research, it is important to know where to find records, because these are not necessarily in the obvious place, the local county record office. The general principles about the whereabouts of archives need to be understood, in the first place. Church records in England and Wales are organized by dioceses which are not always the same as counties, although the majority of county record offices are in fact diocesan record offices as well. These are of primary importance since as well as parish registers and bishops' transcripts, wills were proved in church courts, and so are in diocesan archives. The records of the central government, including the armed forces, national courts, taxation, and the superior probate court, are in the Public Record Office, in London, while records of local administration like county quarter session courts are in county record offices. Many landowners are depositing their estate records in county record offices, but it is important to appreciate that some of these people owned property in several counties, and then generally their archives will be in the county where they lived, rather than the more obvious county where the land was. Another complication is the creation of new counties in 1974, which is confusing as earlier records tend to be kept according to the old counties. The maps on pages 136 and 137 show the old and new boundaries, and the list below is cross-referenced according to this.

In Scotland, the majority of archives of all types are collected centrally in Edinburgh, in two adjoining buildings, the Scottish Record Office and West Register House. In Ireland most records which have been brought into archive repositories are in the various offices and libraries in Dublin and Belfast, and in both the Channel Islands and the Isle of Man, archives are generally centralized. It is important to remember that many church records are still held in the churches and chapels, in the custody of the respective clergymen, particularly in Ireland. Access to these records is not an automatic right for researchers, and their custodians have more important duties than accommodating family historians, who should remember the courtesies of both a prior appointment and a donation to church funds.

Anyone visiting a record office or library should acquaint themselves in the first place with whether the records in question are at that place, and also to confirm their availability. Opening hours may vary and in some places a prior appointment or reservation of a seat is necessary. The following is a list of useful guides to locating archives.

Record Repositories

Record Repositories in Great Britain (HM Stationery Office, London, 8th edition 1987) lists addresses, opening hours, and principal categories of archives held at each repository. It also lists any guides published to the individual record offices. In particular . the *Guide to the Contents of the Public Record Office* (HM Stationery Office, London, 3 volumes 1963–1968) is important and can be found at most reference libraries.

Parish Registers

Original Parish Registers in Record Offices and Libraries (Local Population Studies, Matlock, 1974, with periodical supplements). This series of booklets lists original Church of England registers which have been deposited in record offices and libraries, only.

National Index of Parish Registers (Society of Genealogists, in progress, 12 volumes). When completed this will list details of all parish and other registers, and copies of indexes of them, in Great Britain, but much remains to be completed.

Guide to the Parish and Non-Parochial Registers of Devon and Cornwall 1538–1837 (Devon and Cornwall Record Society, 1979). A comprehensive guide with maps.

Parish Register Copies Part One – Society of Genealogists Collection and *Parish Register Copies Part Two – Other than the Society of Genealogists Collection* (Society of Genealogists, London) list copies of parish registers and their whereabouts.

In addition many county and other record offices publish lists of registers in their custody.

Wills

A. J. Camp's *Wills and their Whereabouts* (privately published, 1974) and J. S. W. Gibson's *Wills and Where to Find Them* (Chichester, 1974) are comprehensive guides but are both out of print. J. S. W. Gibson's *A Simplified Guide to Probate Jurisdictions* (Gulliver Press and the Federation of Family History Societies, 1980) is in print and is an adequate brief guide.

Manorial Records and other Landowners' Archives

There is no published guide but the Historical Manuscripts Commission maintains the Manorial Documents Register and the National Register of Archives, which list the whereabouts of such material where it is known. The indexes and catalogues may be consulted at Quality House, Quality Court, Chancery Lane, London WC2A 1HP.

Other Sources

Federation of Family History Societies Handbook lists addresses of all family history societies in the British Isles, and is obtainable from the Secretary, c/o The Administrator, Benson Room, Birmingham and Midland Institute, Margaret Street, Birmingham B3 3BS. The Federation of Family History Societies and Gulliver Press publish jointly *Census Returns 1841, 1851, 1861, 1871 on Microfilm: a Directory to Local Holdings; Marriage Indexes: How to Find Them, How to Use Them, How to Compile One; Bishops' Transcripts and Marriage Licences: A Guide to their Location and Indexes*.

The following list of record offices and libraries is not necessarily complete but includes those of most significance, in particular diocesan record offices and genealogical libraries. Cross-references reflect county boundary changes in 1974, and the evolution of Greater London, but ignore other earlier changes of county boundaries.

From the autumn of 1987 most county record offices required searchers to obtain a reader's ticket. The need to acquire and carry a ticket may seem to be an irritating piece of bureaucracy, but it has become increasingly necessary to preserve archival material. With the rise in the market value of certain documents some serious thefts have taken place. Readers' tickets are part of a programme to increase security. A research network has been set up to help those who use more than one county record office. Instead of a ticket for each office, issued in different ways to different rules, a single ticket, which can be obtained from any of the participating offices, will give access to them all. However, *not all record offices have joined the network*, and before embarking on a journey searchers should check what the local rules and requirements are. Those offices participating in the network in 1988 were Berkshire, Buckinghamshire, Cambridgeshire, Cleveland Archives Department, Cornwall, Cumbria, East Sussex, Essex, Greater Manchester Record Office, Gwent, Hampshire, Hereford and Worcester Record Office, Hertfordshire, Kent, Lancashire, Norfolk, Northumberland, Nottinghamshire, Suffolk (East and West), Wiltshire.

APPENDIX V: RECORD OFFICES, LIBRARIES AND SOCIETIES

Searchers should obtain a copy of the leaflet *County Archive Research Network* from any of the above record offices. HM Stationery Office issues periodical lists of addresses of local record offices, which should be consulted in case of difficulty or doubt.

England

Avon (see also Gloucestershire; Somerset)

Bath City Record Office, Guildhall, Bath BA1 5AW
Tel (0225) 61111 Ext 201

Bath Reference Library, 18 Queen Square, Bath BA1 2HP
Tel (0225) 28144

Bristol Record Office, Council House, College Green, Bristol BS1 5TR   Tel (0272) 266031 Ext 442

Bedfordshire

Bedfordshire Record Office, County Hall, Bedford MK42 9AP
Tel (0234) 228833/63222 Ext 2833

Berkshire (see also Buckinghamshire; Oxfordshire)

Berkshire Record Office, Shire Hall, Shinfield Park, Reading
RG2 9XD   Tel (0734) 875444 Ext 3182

Buckinghamshire (see also Berkshire)

Buckinghamshire Record Office, County Hall, Aylesbury HP20 1UA   Tel (0296) 395000 Ext 587

Buckinghamshire Archaeological Society, County Museum, Church Street, Aylesbury HP20 2QP

Cambridgeshire (includes former county of Huntingdonshire; see also Northamptonshire)

Cambridgeshire County Record Office, Shire Hall, Castle Hill, Cambridge CB3 0AP   Tel (0223) 317281

Cambridgeshire Record Office, Grammar School Walk, Huntingdon PE18 6LF   Tel (0480) 425842

Cambridge University Library, Department of Manuscripts, West Road, Cambridge CB3 9DR   Tel (0223) 337733 Ext 3143

Cambridge University Archives   Tel (0223) 337733 Ext 3143

Trinity College Library, Trinity College, Cambridge CB1 1TQ
Tel (0223) 338488

Cheshire (see also Derbyshire; Greater Manchester)

Cheshire Record Office, Duke Street, Chester CH1 1RL
Tel (0244) 602574

Warrington Library, Museum Street, Warrington WA1 1JB
Tel (0925) 571232

Chester Archaeological Society, Chester City Record Office, Town Hall, Chester CH1 2HF   Tel (0244) 324324

Chester City Record Office, Town Hall, Chester CH1 2HF Tel (0244) 324324 Ext 2108

Cleveland (see also Durham; North Yorkshire)

Cleveland County Archives Department, Exchange House, 6 Marton Road, Middlesbrough TS1 1DB   Tel (0642) 248321

Cornwall

Cornwall Record Office, County Hall, Truro TR1 3AY Tel (0872) 73698/74282 Ext 3127

Royal Institution of Cornwall, County Museum, River Street, Truro TR1 2SJ   Tel (0872) 72205

Cumberland (see Cumbria)

Cumbria (includes Cumberland, Westmorland, parts of Lancashire and Yorkshire)

Cumbria Record Office, The Castle, Carlisle CA3 8UR Tel (0228) 23456 Ext 2416

Cumbria Record Office, County Offices, Kendal LA9 4RQ Tel (0539) 21000 Ext 329

Cumbria Record Office, 140 Duke Street, Barrow-in-Furness LA14 1XW   Tel (0229) 31269

Derbyshire (see also Cheshire)

Derbyshire Record Office, County Offices, Matlock DE4 3AG Tel (0629) 580000 Ext 7347

Devon

Devon Record Office, Castle Street, Exeter EX4 3PU Tel (0392) 273509

Devon and Cornwall Record Society, 7 The Close, Exeter EX1 1EZ   Tel (0392) 74727

Exeter Cathedral Library, Old Bishop's Palace, Diocesan House, Palace Gate, Exeter EX1 1HX   Tel (0392) 72894

West Devon Record Office, Unit 3, Clare Place, Coxside, Plymouth PL4 0JW   Tel (0752) 264685

Dorset (see also Hampshire)

Dorset Record Office, County Hall, Dorchester DT1 1XJ Tel (0305) 204411/251000

APPENDIX V: RECORD OFFICES, LIBRARIES AND SOCIETIES

Durham (see also Cleveland; Tyne and Wear; Yorkshire)

Durham County Record Office, County Hall, Durham DH1 5UL
Tel 091-386 4411 Ext 2474/2253

Dean and Chapter Library, The College, Durham DH1 3EH
Tel 091-386 2489

Department of Palaeography and Diplomatic, The Prior's
Kitchen, The College, Durham DH1 3EQ   Tel 091-374 3615/6

Durham University Library, Department of Special Collections,
Palace Green, Durham DH1 3RN   Tel 091-374 3018 Ext 411/457

Essex (see also Greater London)

Essex Record Office, County Hall, Chelmsford CM1 1LX
Tel (0245) 267222 Ext 2104

Essex Record Office, Colchester and North-East Essex Branch,
Stanwell House, Stanwell Street, Colchester CO2 7DL
Tel (0206) 572099

Essex Record Office, Southend Branch, Central Library, Victoria
Avenue, Southend-on-Sea SS2 6EX   Tel (0702) 612621

Gloucestershire (see also Avon)

Gloucestershire Record Office, Clarence Row, off Alvin Street,
Gloucester GL1 3DW   Tel (0452) 425295

Hampshire (see also Dorset; Isle of Wight)

Hampshire Record Office, 20 Southgate Street, Winchester SO23
9EF   Tel (0962) 63153

Portsmouth City Records Office, 3 Museum Road, Portsmouth
PO1 2LE   Tel (0705) 829765

Southampton City Record Office, Civic Centre, Southampton
SO9 4XR   Tel (0703) 832251/223855 Ext 2251

Hereford and Worcester (see also West Midlands)

Hereford and Worcester Record Office, County Hall, Spetchley
Road, Worcester WR5 2NP   Tel (0905) 353366 Ext 3615

Hereford Record Office, The Old Barracks, Harold Street,
Hereford HR1 2QX   Tel (0432) 265441

Worcester (St Helen's) Record Office, Fish Street, Worcester
WR1 2HW   Tel (0905) 353366 Ext 3616

Hertfordshire (see also Greater London)

Hertfordshire Record Office, County Hall, Hertford SG13 8DE
Tel (0992) 555105

APPENDIX V: RECORD OFFICES, LIBRARIES AND SOCIETIES

Humberside (see also Lincolnshire; Yorkshire)

Humberside County Record Office, County Hall, Beverley HU17 9BA   Tel (0482) 867131 Ext 3394

South Humberside Area Record Office, Town Hall Square, Grimsby DN31 1HX   Tel (0472) 353481

Kingston upon Hull City Record Office, 79 Lowgate, Hull HU1 2AA   Tel (0482) 222015/6

Huntingdonshire (see Cambridgeshire)

Kent (see also Greater London)

Kent Archives Office, County Hall, Maidstone ME14 1XQ
Tel (0622) 671411 Ext 3363

Kent Archives Office, North East Kent Area, Ramsgate Library, Guildford Lawn, Ramsgate CT11 9AI   Tel (0843) 593532 Ext 3

Kent Archives Office, South East Kent Area, Central Library, Grace Hill, Folkestone CT20 1HD   Tel (0303) 57583

Canterbury Cathedral, City and Diocesan Record Office, The Precincts, Canterbury CT1 2EG   Tel (0227) 463510

Lancashire (see also Cumbria; Greater Manchester; Merseyside)

Lancashire Record Office, Bow Lane, Preston PR1 8ND
Tel (0772) 54868 Ext 3039/3041

Leicestershire (includes Rutland)

Leicestershire Record Office, 57 New Walk, Leicester LE1 7JB
Tel (0533) 544566

Lincolnshire (see also Humberside)

Lincolnshire Archives Office, The Castle, Lincoln LN1 3AB
Tel (0522) 25158

Greater London

Record offices and libraries in Greater London are a complex subject and, being the capital, it is not always possible to draw a clear distinction between local and national archives. The following list is not necessarily complete and deliberately omits repositories of minor importance. There are many specialist societies and libraries, and local reference libraries not in this list but which may be of value for individual and specialist needs.

NATIONAL AND GENERAL ARCHIVES AND LIBRARIES

Army Records Centre, Bourne Avenue, Hayes, Middlesex UB3 1RF   Tel 081-573 3831 Ext 334

APPENDIX V: RECORD OFFICES, LIBRARIES AND SOCIETIES

British Library Department of Western Manuscripts, Great Russell Street, London WC1B 3DG
Tel 071-636 1544, 071-928 9531

British Records Association, Master's Court, The Charterhouse, Charterhouse Square, London EC1M 6AU   Tel 071-253 0436

Business Archives Council, 185 Tower Bridge Road, London SE1 2UF   Tel 071-407 6110

Church House Record Centre, Church House, Dean's Yard, London SW1P 3NZ   Tel 071-222 9011 Ext 203

College of Arms, Queen Victoria Street, London EC4V 4BT
Tel 071-248 2762

House of Lords Record Office, House of Lords, London SW1A 0PW   Tel 071-219 3074

Imperial War Museum, Department of Documents, Lambeth Road, London SE1 6HZ   Tel 071-735 8922

Lambeth Palace Library, London SE1 7JU   Tel 071-928 6222

National Army Museum, Department of Records, Royal Hospital Road, London SW3 4HT   Tel 071-730 0717 Ext 47

National Maritime Museum, Manuscripts Section, Greenwich, London SE10 9NF   Tel 081-858 4422

Census Office, General Register Office, St Catherine's House, 10 Kingsway, London WC2B 6JP   Tel 071-242 0262 Ext 2446

Probate Office, Somerset House, Strand, London WC2R 1LP
Tel 071-936 6960

Public Record Office, Chancery Lane, London WC2A 1LR
(*Medieval, Legal, Probate and Nonconformist records*)
Tel 071-405 0741

Public Record Office, Portugal Street, London WC2A 3PH
(*Census Records*)   Tel 071-405 3488 Ext 335

Public Record Office, Ruskin Avenue, Kew, Richmond TW9 4DU (*Departmental Records*)   Tel 081-876 3444

Royal Air Force Museum, Department of Aviation Records (Archives), Aerodrome Road, Hendon, London NW9 5LL
Tel 081-205 2266 Ext 210/211

Royal Commission on Historical Manuscripts, Quality House, Quality Court, Chancery Lane, London WC2A 1HP
Tel 071-242 1198

Society of Genealogists, 14 Charterhouse Buildings, Goswell Road, London EC1M 7BA   Tel 071-251 8799

APPENDIX V: RECORD OFFICES, LIBRARIES AND SOCIETIES

Greater London Record Office, 40 Northampton Road, London EC1R 0HB   Tel 071-633 6851

Corporation of London Records Office, PO Box 270, Guildhall, London EC2P 2EJ   Tel 071-606 3030 Ext 1251

Guildhall Library, Aldermanbury, London EC2P 2EJ Tel 071-606 3030 Ext 1863

Bexley Libraries and Museums Department, Local Studies Section, Hall Place, Bourne Road, Bexley DA5 1PQ Tel (0322) 526574 Ext 217/218

Bromley Public Libraries, Archives Section, Central Library, High Street, Bromley BR1 1EX   Tel 081-460 9955 Ext 261

Camden Public Libraries, Local History Library, Swiss Cottage Library, 88 Avenue Road, London NW3 3HA Tel 071-586 5989 Ext 234

Camden Public Libraries, Local History Library, Holborn Library, 32–38 Theobalds Road, London WC1X 8PA Tel 071-405 2706 Ext 337

Greenwich Local History Library, Woodlands, 90 Mycenae Road, Blackheath, London SE3 7SE   Tel 081-858 4631

Hackney Archives Department, Rose Lipman Library, De Beauvoir Road, London N1 5SQ   Tel 071-241 2886

Hammersmith and Fulham Archives, Shepherd's Bush Library, 7 Uxbridge Road, London W12 8LJ Tel 081-743 0910/081-748 3020 Ext 3850

Haringey Libraries, Museum and Arts Department, Bruce Castle Museum, Lordship Lane, London N17 8NU   Tel 081-808 8772

Kensington and Chelsea Libraries and Arts Service, Central Library, Phillimore Walk, London W8 7RX Tel 071-937 2542 Ext 3038/3004

Lambeth Archives Department, Minet Library, 52 Knatchbull Road, London SE5 9QY   Tel 071-733 3279

Lewisham Local History Centre, The Manor House, Old Road, London SE13 5SY   Tel 081-852 5050

Redbridge Central Library, Local History Room, Clements Road, Ilford EG1 1EA   Tel 081-478 7145

Southwark Local Studies Library, 211 Borough High Street, London SE1 1JA   Tel 071-403 3507

Tower Hamlets Libraries, Local History Library, 277 Bancroft Road, London E1 4DQ   Tel 081-980 4366 Ext 47

Waltham Forest Archives, Vestry House Museum, Vestry Road, Walthamstow, London E17 9NH   Tel 081-509 1917/081-527 4391

Westminster City Libraries, Archives Section, Victoria Library, 160 Buckingham Palace Road, London SW1W 9UD
Tel 071-798 2180

King's College London, Liddell Hart Centre for Military Archives, Strand, London WC2R 2LS   Tel 071-836 5454 Ext 2187

University College London, Manuscripts Room, The Library, Gower Street, London WC1E 6BT   Tel 071-387 7050 Ext 2617/8

Royal College of Physicians of London, 11 St Andrews Place, London NW1 4LE   Tel 071-935 1174

Royal College of Surgeons of England, 35–43 Lincoln's Inn Fields, London WC2A 3PN   Tel 071-405 3474 Ext 8

Society of Antiquaries of London, Burlington House, Piccadilly, LondonW1V 0HS   Tel 071-734 0193/071-437 9954

Westminster Abbey Muniment Room and Library, London SW1P 3PA   Tel 071-222 5152 Ext 228

Greater Manchester (see also Cheshire; Lancashire; Yorkshire)

Greater Manchester County Record Office, 56 Marshall Street, New Cross, Manchester M4 5FU   Tel 061-247 3383

John Rylands University Library, Deansgate, Manchester M3 3EH   Tel 061-834 5343

Manchester Central Library, Archives Department, St Peter's Square, Manchester M2 5PD   Tel 061-236 9422 Ext 269

Bolton Archive Service, Central Library, Civic Centre, Le Mans Crescent, Bolton BL1 1SE   Tel (0204) 22311 Ext 2179

Bury Archive Service, 112 The Rock, Bury BL9 0PD
Tel 061-764 8625

Rochdale Libraries, Local Studies Department, Area Central Library, Esplanade, Rochdale OL16 1AQ
Tel (0706) 47474 Ext 423

Salford Archives Centre, 658/662 Liverpool Road, Irlam, Manchester M30 5AD   Tel 061-775 5643

Stockport Archive Service, Central Library, Wellington Road South, Stockport, SK1 3RS   Tel 061-480 7297/3038

Tameside Local Studies Library, Stalybridge Library, Trinity Street, Stalybridge SK15 2BN   Tel 061-338 2708/3831

Wigan Record Office, Town Hall, Leigh WN7 2DY
Tel (0942) 672421 Ext 266

Merseyside (see also Cheshire; Lancashire)

Liverpool Record Office and Local History Department, City
Libraries, William Brown Street, Liverpool L3 8EW
Tel 051-207 2147 Ext 34

Maritime Records Centre, Merseyside Maritime Museum, Pier
Head, Liverpool L3 1DN   Tel 051-709 1551 Ext 218

St Helens Local History and Archives Library, Central Library,
Gamble Institute, Victoria Square, St Helens WA10 1DY
Tel (0744) 24061 Ext 2952

Wirral Archives Service, Birkenhead Reference Library, Borough
Road, Birkenhead L41 2XB   Tel 051-652 6106/7/8 Ext 34

West Midlands (see also Staffordshire; Warwickshire; Worcestershire)

Birmingham Central Libraries, Archive Department,
Chamberlain Square, Birmingham B3 3HQ   Tel 021-235 4217

Coventry City Record Office, Mandela House, Bayley Lane,
Coventry CV1 5RG   Tel (0203) 25555 Ext 2768

Dudley Archives and Local History Department, Dudley Library,
St James's Road, Dudley DY9 9EL
Tel (0384) 55433 Ext 5514/5526

Walsall Archives Service, Local History Centre, Essex Street,
Walsall WS2 7AS   Tel (0922) 37305/6

Wolverhampton Borough Archives, Central Library, Snow Hill,
Wolverhampton WV1 3AX   Tel (0902) 312025 Ext 37

Middlesex (see Greater London)

Norfolk

Norfolk Record Office, Central Library, Norwich NR2 1NJ
Tel (0603) 611277 Ext 262

Northamptonshire (see also Cambridgeshire)

Northamptonshire Record Office, Delapré Abbey, London Road,
Northampton NN4 9AW   Tel (0604) 762129

Northumberland (see also Tyne and Wear)

Northumberland Record Office, Melton Park, North Gosforth,
Newcastle upon Tyne NE3 5QX   Tel 091-236 2680

Nottinghamshire (see also Yorkshire)

Nottinghamshire Record Office, County House, High Pavement,
Nottingham NG1 1HR   Tel (0602) 504524

Oxfordshire (see also Berkshire)

Oxfordshire County Record Office, County Hall, New Road, Oxford OX1 1ND   Tel (0865) 815203

Bodleian Library, Department of Western Manuscripts, Oxford OX1 3BG   Tel (0865) 277000 Ext 286

Manchester College Library (*Unitarian biographies*), Mansfield Road, Oxford OX1 3TD   Tel (0865) 241514

Rhodes House Library, South Parks Road, Oxford OX1 3RG Tel (0865) 270909

Rutland (see Leicestershire; Northamptonshire)

Salop (see Shropshire)

Shropshire

Shropshire Record Office, Shirehall, Abbey Foregate, Shrewsbury SY2 6ND   Tel (0743) 252851/3

Somerset (see also Avon)

Somerset Record Office, Obridge Road, Taunton TA2 7PU Tel (0823) 337600

Staffordshire (see also West Midlands)

Staffordshire Record Office, Eastgate Street, Stafford ST16 2LZ Tel (0785) 223121 Ext 8380

Lichfield Joint Record Office, Lichfield Library, Bird Street, Lichfield WS13 6PN   Tel (0543) 256787

William Salt Library, Eastgate Street, Stafford ST16 2LZ Tel (0785) 52276

Suffolk (see also Norfolk)

Suffolk Record Office, County Hall, Ipswich IP4 2JS Tel (0473) 230000 Ext 4235

Suffolk Record Office, Bury St Edmunds Branch, Raingate Street, Bury St Edmunds IP33 1RX   Tel (0284) 63141 Ext 2522

Suffolk Record Office, Lowestoft Branch, Central Library, Clapham Road, Lowestoft NR32 1DR   Tel (0502) 66325 Ext 274

Surrey (see also Greater London)

Surrey Record Office, County Hall, Penrhyn Road, Kingston upon Thames KT1 2DN   Tel 081-541 9065

Surrey Record Office, Guildford Muniment Room, Castle Arch, Guildford GU1 3SX   Tel (0483) 573942

Army Museums Ogilby Trust, Connaught Barracks, Duke of

Connaught's Road, Aldershot GU11 2LR
Tel (0252) 24431 Ext 2895

East Sussex (see also West Sussex)

East Sussex Record Office, The Maltings, Castle Precincts, Lewes
BN7 1YT Tel (0273) 475400 Ext 12/359

West Sussex (see also East Sussex)

West Sussex Record Office, County Hall, Chichester PO19 1RN
Tel (0243) 777983

Tyne and Wear (see also Durham; Northumberland)

Tyne and Wear Archives Service, Blandford House, West
Blandford Street, Newcastle upon Tyne NE1 4JA Tel 091-232
6789

Warwickshire (see also West Midlands)

Warwick County Record Office, Priory Park, Cape Road,
Warwick CV34 4JS Tel (0926) 493431 Ext 2508

Westmorland (see Cumbria)

Isle of Wight (see also Hampshire)

Isle of Wight County Record Office, 26 Hillside, Newport PO30
2EB Tel (0983) 524031 Ext 132/3

Wiltshire

Wiltshire Record Office, County Hall, Trowbridge BA14 8JG
Tel (0225) 753641 Ext 3502

Salisbury District Council Muniment Room, Council House,
Bourne Hill, Salisbury Tel (0722) 33627

Worcestershire (see Hereford and Worcester; West Midlands)

Yorkshire

Prior to 1974, this county was divided into three Ridings, North,
East, and West. By the changes made in 1974, the county of
Humberside takes in most of the former East Riding, together with
part of Lincolnshire; the county of Cleveland takes in part of the
former North Riding, together with part of county Durham; the
county of North Yorkshire includes the remainder of the former
North Riding, apart from a small area transferred to Cumbria,
together with the northern part of the former West Riding, and the
remainder of the former East Riding; the remainder of the former
West Riding now forms the two counties of South Yorkshire and
West Yorkshire (the former taking in also a small part of former
Nottinghamshire), apart from small areas transferred to Lancashire
and Greater Manchester.

North Yorkshire

North Yorkshire County Record Office, County Hall, Northallerton DL7 8AD   Tel (0609) 780780 Ext 3902

York University, Borthwick Institute of Historical Research, St Anthony's Hall, Peasholme Green, York YO1 2PW Tel (0904) 642315

York City Archives Department, Art Gallery Buildings, Exhibition Square, York YO1 2EW   Tel (0904) 51533

York Minster Library, Dean's Park, York YO1 2JD Tel (0904) 25308

South Yorkshire

Barnsley Archive Service, Central Library, Shambles Street, Barnsley S70 2JF   Tel (0226) 283241 Ext 23

Doncaster Archives Department, King Edward Road, Balby, Doncaster DN4 0NA   Tel (0302) 859811

Sheffield Record Office, Central Library, Surrey Street, Sheffield S1 1XZ   Tel (0742) 734756

West Yorkshire

West Yorkshire Archives, Headquarters and Wakefield, Registry of Deeds, Newstead Road, Wakefield WF1 2DE Tel (0924) 367111 Ext 2352

West Yorkshire Archives, Bradford, 15 Canal Road, Bradford BD1 4AT   Tel (0274) 731931

West Yorkshire Archives, Calderdale, Central Library, Northgate House, Northgate, Halifax HX1 1UN   Tel (0422) 57257 Ext 2636

West Yorkshire Archives, Kirklees, Central Library, Princess Alexandra Walk, Huddersfield HD1 2SU Tel (0484) 513808 Ext 207

West Yorkshire Archives, Leeds, Chapeltown Road, Sheepscar, Leeds LS7 3AP   Tel (0532) 628339

Leeds University, Brotherton Library, Leeds LS2 9JT Tel (0532) 431751 Ext 7278

Yorkshire Archaeological Society, Claremont, 23 Clarendon Road, Leeds LS2 9NZ   Tel (0532) 456362

Wales

Wales now includes the former county of Monmouthshire, which was formerly part of England. Until recent years the National Library of Wales, Aberystwyth, was the principal repository, and the only one authorized for church records. Although local record offices have now been established, the National Library remains predominant, and *inter alia* holds all probate records and bishops' transcripts. Welsh counties have also been reorganized; the former counties of Cardigan, Carmarthen and Pembroke now form the single county of Dyfed; the former county of Glamorgan, together with small parts of Brecon and Monmouth, forms the three new counties of West, Mid and South Glamorgan which are served by a single record office; the remainder of Monmouthshire is now called Gwent; the remainder of Breconshire, with Radnorshire and Montgomeryshire, forms the new county of Powys; Flintshire, most of Denbighshire, and a small part of Merioneth form the new county of Clwyd; and finally Anglesey, Caernarvonshire, the remainder of Merioneth and a small part of Denbighshire form the new county of Gwynedd.

Clwyd

Clwyd Record Office, Hawarden Branch, The Old Rectory, Hawarden, Deeside CH5 3NR   Tel (0244) 532364

Clwyd Record Office, Ruthin Branch, 46 Clwyd Street, Ruthin LL15 1HP   Tel (082 42) 3077

Dyfed

National Library of Wales, Department of Manuscripts and Records, Aberystwyth SY23 3BU   Tel (0970) 323816

Dyfed Archives Service, Carmarthenshire Area Record Office, County Hall, Camarthen SA31 1JP   Tel (0267) 233333 Ext 4184

Cardiganshire Area Record Office, County Office, Marine Terrace, Aberystwyth SY23 2DE   Tel (0970) 617581 Ext 2120

Pembrokeshire Area Record Office, The Castle, Haverfordwest SA61 2EF   Tel (0437) 763707

Glamorgan, Mid, South, and West

Glamorgan Archive Service (for Mid, South and West Glamorgan), Glamorgan Record Office, County Hall, Cathays Park, Cardiff CF1 3NE   Tel (0222) 820282

West Glamorgan Area Record Office, County Hall, Oystermouth Road, Swansea SA1 3SN   Tel (0792) 471589

Gwent

Gwent County Record Office, County Hall, Cwmbran NP44 2XH   Tel (06333) 838838

Gwynedd

Gwynedd Archives and Museums Service, Caernarfon Area

Record Office, Victoria Dock, Caernarfon LL55 1SH
Tel (0286) 679095 Ext 2095

Dolgellau Area Record Office, Cae Penarlag, Dolgellau LL40
2YB   Tel (0341) 422341 Ext 261

Llangefni Area Record Office, Shire Hall, Llangefni LL77 7TW
Tel (0248) 750262 Ext 269

University College of North Wales Library, Department of
Manuscripts, Bangor LL57 2DG   Tel (0248) 351151 Ext 316

Powys

Powys Library Headquarters, Archives,Cefnllys Road,
Llandrindod Wells LD1 5LD   Tel (0597) 826060

Scotland

Although regional and other archives have been formed recently
outside Edinburgh, in general these hold specialized material which
will be needed only when that in Edinburgh has been exhausted.

Scottish Record Office, HM General Register House, Princes
Street, Edinburgh EH1 3YY   Tel 031-556 6585

Scottish Record Office, West Register House, Charlotte Square,
Edinburgh EH2 4DF   Tel 031-556 6585 Ext 287

The General Register Office (Scotland), New Register House,
West Register Street, Edinburgh EH1 3YT   Tel 031-556 3952

Business Archives Council of Scotland, Glasgow University
Archives, The University, Glasgow G12 8QQ
Tel 041-339 8855 Ext 5515/6

Central

Central Regional Council Archives Department, Old High
School, Spittal Street, Stirling FK8 1DG
Tel (0786) 73111 Ext 466

Dumfries and Galloway

Dumfries and Galloway Regional Library Service, Ewart Public
Library, Catherine Street, Dumfries DG1 1JB   Tel (0387) 53820

Dumfries Archive Centre, 33 Burns Street, Dumfries DG1 2PS
Tel (0387) 69254

Fife

St Andrews University Library, North Street, St Andrews KY16
9TR   Tel (0334) 76161 Ext 514

Grampian

Grampian Regional Archives, Old Aberdeen House, Dunbar

Street, Aberdeen AB2 1UE   Tel (0224) 481775

Moray District Record Office, Tolbooth, High Street, Forres IV36 0AB   Tel (0309) 73617

Aberdeen City Archives, Town House, Aberdeen AB9 1AQ Tel (0224) 642121 Ext 513

Highland

Highland Regional Archive, The Library, Farraline Park, InvernessIV1 1NH   Tel (0463) 236463

Lothian

National Library of Scotland, Department of Manuscripts, George IV Bridge, Edinburgh EH1 1EW   Tel 031-226 4531

City of Edinburgh District Council Archives, Department of Administration, City Chambers, High Street, Edinburgh EH1 1YJ Tel 031-225 2424 Ext 5196

Scottish Catholic Archives, Columba House, 16 Drummond Place, Edinburgh EH3 6PL   Tel 031-556 3661

Orkney

Orkney Archives, The Orkney Library, Laing Street, Kirkwall KW15 1NW   Tel (0856) 873166 Ext 5

Shetland

Shetland Archives, 44 King Harald Street, Lerwick ZE1 0EQ Tel (0595) 3535 Ext 269

Strathclyde

Strathclyde Regional Archives, Mitchell Library, North Street, Glasgow G3 7DN   Tel 041-227 2401/5

Argyll and Bute District Archives, Argyll and Bute District Council, Kilmory, Lochgilphead PA31 8RT Tel (0546) 602127 Ext 120

City of Glasgow, Mitchell Library, North Street, Glasgow G3 7DN   Tel 041-221 7030 Ext 171

Glasgow University Library, Special Collections Department, Hillhead Street, Glasgow G12 8QE   Tel 041-339 8855 Ext 6767

Ayrshire Sub Regional Archives, County Buildings, Wellington Square, Ayrshire   Tel 041-227 2401/5

Tayside

Dundee District Archive and Record Centre, City Chambers, City Square, Dundee DD1 3BY   Tel (0382) 23141 Ext 4494

Perth and Kinross District Archive, Sandeman Library, 16

Kinnoull Street, Perth, PH1 5ET   Tel (0738) 23329

The Isle of Man

General Registry, Finch Road, Douglas   Tel (0624) 75506

Manx Museum Library, Kingswood Grove, Douglas
Tel (0624) 75522/25125 Ext 133

The Channel Islands

Alderney

Clerk of the States, Queen Elizabeth II Street, Alderney
Tel (048 182) 2816

Guernsey

Greffe, Royal Court House, St Peter Port, Guernsey
Tel (0481) 25277

La Société Guernesiaise, Candy Gardens, St Peter Port, Guernsey
Tel (0481) 21915

Jersey

Judicial Greffe, 10 Hill Street, St Helier, Jersey   Tel (0534) 75472

La Société Jersiaise, Museum and Library, 9 Pier Road, St Helier,
Jersey   Tel (0534) 75940

Sark

The Greffier, Sark   Tel (048 183) 2012

Ireland
(including Northern Ireland and the Republic of Ireland)

Although Northern Ireland (part of the United Kingdom) and the
Republic of Ireland (Eire) have been politically separate from
1922, their former union means that their archives are not separate.
In particular many archives relating to Northern Ireland are in the
Republic, and the reverse applies to a lesser extent.

Northern Ireland

Public Record Office of Northern Ireland, 66 Balmoral Avenue,
Belfast BT9 6NY   Tel (0232) 661621/663286

General Register Office (Northern Ireland), Oxford House, 49–55
Chichester Street, Belfast BT1 4HL
Tel (0232) 235211 Ext 2329/2326

Presbyterian Historical Society, Assembly House, Fisherwick
Place, Belfast   Tel (0232) 32396

Friends Meeting House, Lisburn, Co Antrim

Republic of Ireland

General Register Office, 8 Lombard Street East, Dublin 2
Tel (0001) 711000

National Archives, Four Courts, Dublin 7   Tel (0001) 733833

National Library of Ireland, Kildare Street, Dublin 2
Tel (0001) 618811

Registry of Deeds, King's Inn, Henrietta Street, Dublin 1
Tel (0001) 733300

Genealogical Office, Kildare Street, Dublin 2   Tel (0001) 614877

State Paper Office, Dublin Castle, Dublin 2   Tel (0001) 792777

Royal Irish Academy, 19 Dawson Street, Dublin 2
Tel (0001) 762570

Trinity College Library, Trinity College, College Green, Dublin 2
Tel (0001) 772941

Library of the Church Representative Body, Braemor Park,
Dublin 14   Tel (0001) 979979

The Religious Society of Friends in Ireland, Swanbrook House,
Morehampton Road, Dublin 4   Tel (0001) 687157

Irish Manuscripts Commission, 73 Merrion Square, Dublin 2
Tel (0001) 689333

Cork Archives Council, Christchurch South Main Street, Cork
Tel (010 35 321) 277809

Miscellaneous National

(See also under Greater London)

Association of Genealogists and Record Agents, 29 Badgers
Close, Horsham, West Sussex RH12 5RU

Federation of Family History Societies, c/o The Administrator,
Benson Room, Birmingham and Midland Institute, Margaret
Street, Birmingham B3 3BS

Society of Genealogists, 14 Charterhouse Buildings, Goswell
Road, London EC1M 7BA   Tel 071-251 8799

Religious Denominational Archives

Baptist Union Library, Baptist House, 129 Broadway, Didcot,
Oxon OX11 8RT

Catholic Central Library, 47 Francis Street, London SW1P 1QR
Tel 071-834 6128

Catholic Record Society, 114 Mount Street, London W1Y 6AH

Congregational Library, 14 Gordon Square, London WC1H 0AG
Tel 071-387 3727

APPENDIX V: RECORD OFFICES, LIBRARIES AND SOCIETIES

Dr Williams Library, 14 Gordon Square, London WC1H 0AG
Tel 071-387 3727

Huguenot Library, University College, Gower Street, London
WC1E 6BP   Tel 071-380 7094

Jewish Museum, Woburn House, Upper Woburn Place, London
WC1 0EP   Tel 071-388 4525

Methodist Archives and Research Centre (*obituaries only*), John
Rylands University Library, Deansgate, Manchester M3 3EH
Tel 061-834 5343/6765

Presbyterians (see under United Reformed Church)

Society of Friends' Library, Friends House, Euston Road, London
NW1 2BJ   Tel 071-387 3601

Unitarian Church Headquarters, Essex Hall, 1–6 Essex Street,
London WC2R 3HY   Tel 071-240 2384

United Reformed Church Historical Society, 86 Tavistock Place,
London WC1H 9RT   Tel 071-837 7661

Westminster Archiepiscopal Archives (*Roman Catholic*), 16A
Abingdon Road, London W8 6AF   Tel 071-938 3580

Westminster Diocesan Archives, Archbishop's House,
Ambrosden Avenue, London SW1P 1QJ   Tel 071-834 4717

Bibliography

General Sources

J. Cox and T. Padfield *Tracing Your Ancestors in the Public Record Office* 1981
Family Tree Magazine
Federation of Family History Societies *Family History News and Digest*
T. V. H. Fitzhugh *The Dictionary of Genealogy* 1985
J. S. W. Gibson and P. Peskett *Record Offices: How to find them* 1987
L. C. Hector *The Handwriting of English Documents* 1979
D. Hey *Family History and Local History in England* 1987
C. R. Humphery-Smith *Genealogists' Bibliography* 1985
E. McLaughlin *Illegitimacy* 1986
P. Palgrave-Moore *How to Record your Family Tree* 1979
J. Richardson *The Local Historian's Encyclopaedia* 1986
N. A. M. Rodger *Naval Records for Genealogists* 1984
A. Wagner *English Genealogy* 1983
A. J. Willis and M. Tatchell *Genealogy for Beginners* 1984

Parish Records

J. H. Bettey *Church & Parish: A guide for Local Historians* 1987
D. E. Gardner and F. Smith *Genealogical Research in England and Wales* (three volumes) 1956
C. R. Humphery-Smith *The Phillimore Atlas and Index of Parish Registers* 1984
E. McLaughlin *Parish Registers* 1986
D. J. Steel *General sources for births, marriages and deaths before 1837* National Index of Parish Registers
J. S. W. Gibson *Bishops' Transcripts and Marriage Licences, Bonds and Allegations: A guide to their locations and indexes* 1982
G. R. Breed *My Ancestor was a Baptist* 1986
M. Gandy *My Ancestor was Jewish* 1982
W. Leavy *My Ancestor was a Methodist* 1982
E. H. Milligan and M. J. Thomas *My Ancestors were Quakers* 1983
D. J. Steel and E. R. Samuel *Sources for Roman Catholic and Jewish Genealogy and Family History* National Index of Parish Registers Vol 3 1974

Probate Records

A. J. Camp *Wills and their Whereabouts* 1974
J. S. W. Gibson *A Simplified Guide to Probate Jurisdictions* 1985
R. Millward *A Glossary of Household and Farming Terms from 16th c. Probate Inventories* 1979

Quarter Sessions Records

J. S. W. Gibson and D. R. Mills *Land Tax Assessments, c1690–c1950* 1983
J. S. W. Gibson *Quarter Sessions Records for Family Historians* 1983

Miscellaneous Records

M. Audin and N. Currer-Briggs *Nos Ancètres les Anglais* 1983
P. Coldham *English Adventurers and Emigrants 1609–1660* 1984
Cumbria County Council *Cumbrian Ancestors* 1988
N. Currer-Briggs *English Adventurers and Colonial Settlers* 1971
— *English Wills of Colonial Families* 1972
— *The Search for Mr Thomas Kirbye, Gentleman* 1986
— *Virginia Settlers and English Adventurers* 1970
— *Worldwide Family History* 1982
J. S. W. Gibson *Census Returns 1841–1881 on Microfilm* 1983
— *General Register Office and International Genealogical Indexes* 1988
— *The Hearth Tax, Other later Stuart Tax Lists and the Association Oath Rolls* 1985
— *Local Newspapers, 1750–1920 – A Select Location List* 1987
— *Marriage, Census and Other Indexes for Family Historians* 1988
— *Unpublished Personal Name Indexes in Record Offices* 1987
D. Hawgood *Computers for Family History: An Introduction* 1985
K. A. Johnson and M. R. Sainty *Genealogical Research Directory* 1988
J. E. Norton *Guide to the National and Provincial Directories of England and Wales published before 1856* 1950

Acknowledgements

It is impossible for a single author to do justice to a subject as complex as genealogy. We have, therefore, been fortunate in being able to assemble contributions from many specialists, but I must especially thank my colleague, Royston Gambier for his invaluable help in the compilation of this book. His experience both as a practising genealogist and as a teacher, as well as a former chairman and co-founder of the Federation of Family History Societies is of a very special character. Without his assistance and critical attention to detail it would not have been possible to produce this book in the time at our disposal. I am likewise indebted to Hugh Peskett and Charles Teviot for their valuable contributions on Celtic ancestry and on the records of the services and professions as well as to the late Sir Iain Moncreiffe for his thought-provoking Introduction. I must also acknowledge my special gratitude to Peter de V. B. Dewar FSA (Scot) for his valuable assistance in preparing the chapter on heraldry and to Jane Paterson for her contribution on handwriting.

Among the many whom I consulted by letter and through their published works I must thank in particular Margaret Audin, Count Camajani, Professor Hans Eysenck, Sebastian de Ferranti, Francis Leeson, Isobel Mordy, Hugh Montgomery-Massingberd and Edgar Samuel.

I am especially grateful to Susan Quince for typing the manuscript under exceptionally difficult conditions, and to Anne-Marie Ehrlich for her indefatigable help with the illustrations.

Publisher's Note

Picture Credits

Index

INDEX

Barber Surgeons Company 101
Barfoot's London Directory 149
Barmitzvah cards 48
Barrow's *Genealogist's Guide* 51
Báthory, Countess Erszebeth 7
Batavian Republic 125
Bath 89
Baudelaire 32
Becket, Thomas, archbishop 26
Belfast 83, 109, 134, 154
Berkshire 74, 157
Bermuda 97
Bethnal Green 113
Bevis Marks 148
Bible Christian registers 147
Bickley family 72
Birmingham 53
Birmingham & Midland Society for
    Genealogy & Heraldry 1
Birth certificate indexes 56
Birthday books 48
Bishop's transcripts 147
Blythe, Ronald 49
Board of Trade 98
Bodleian Library, Oxford 52, 134
Book plates 48
Borthwick Institute, York 83
Bourbon, Antoine de 18
Bourbon, Charles de 18
Boyle's Street Directory 149
Bradley, Admiral 6
Bradley, Sgt Jonas 6
Breconshire 168
Brecqhou 62
Brian Boru 106
Bristol 113, 119, 120, 139
Britain 120, 124
British army records 123, 124
British Federation of Genealogy
    and Heraldic and Allied
    Societies 1, 2
British Isles 122
British Library 69, 72, 95, 134
British Museum 51, 69, 89
Browning, Robert 32
Brownists, English 118
Brydges, Sir Egerton 27
Buckinghamshire 154
Buckley family 72
Burial in woollen 67, 148
Butler (Boteler) family 46

By-pass Variegated 35

Caen 113
Caernarvonshire 168
Calendar New Style 77
Calendar of State Papers 47, 93
California 117
Calvinist Methodist 148
Cambridge-based Puritans 119
Cambridge Group for the History
    of Population & Social Structure
    69
Cambridge University Library 52,
    134
Cambridgeshire 156
Camp, A. J. 84
Canada 44, 121, 125
Canterbury 112, 135
Canal du Midi 6
Cape Colony 149
Cape Town 125
Capital Taxes Office 85
Cardigan 167
Carmarthen 167
Carolingian Hand 34
Carpathians 7
Casualty Returns 97
Catholic Central Library 172
Caucasus 12
Cavalry muster rolls 148
Cecil family 26, 29
Celtic genealogy 105 et seq
Celtic surnames 42
Cemeteries 71
Census returns 62 et seq
Central America 117
Certificates of Competency 99
Chancery Court 132
Chancery Proceedings 148
Channel Islands 65, 68, 70, 78 et
    seq, 84, 154, 171
Charities 76
Charlemagne 7
Charles I, K. of Gt Britain 15, 32
Charles II, K. of Gt Britain 14, 16,
    18, 91
Charlie, Bonnie prince 7, 14
Chatham 95
Cheshire 1, 83
Chia Pu 11
Chiang Kai-Shek 11

178

Chief Herald of Ireland 52
Children's Act 12
China 11
Chosroes I, II, and III, Ks of
  Armenia 16
Christian names 43
Christianity 118
Church of England 66, 70, 146
Church of Ireland (Protestant) 108
Churchill family 43, 44, 46
Churchill, Sir Winston 7
Churchwardens' Accounts 73
City Chamberlain 102
Civil Registration 55 et seq, 69,
  122, 149
Civil War (English) 91, 120
Clan names 42
Clan system 128
Clergymen 101
Cleveland Archives Dept 156
Close Rolls 88
Clwyd 168
Coastguards 95
Cod-fisheries 119
College of Arms 48, 52, 127 et seq
Collins' peerage 27
Colonies 61
Common Law 107
Common surnames 47
Commonwealth 67, 91
Confucius 11
Congregational (Independent)
  registers 147
Congregational Library 172
Congregationalists 70, 101
Conrad, Joseph 6
Consanguinity 30
Constantine the Thagadir 18
Consular records 60
Continuous Service Engagement
  94
Convict ancestry 124
Convicts 122
Copper-plate hand 34, 35
Copyright Act 52
Cornwall 105, 156
County Councils 75,76
County Libraries 72
County Record Offices 52, 65, 69,
  71, 77, 89, 97, 125, 135
Court hand 34

Court of Common Pleas 132
Court records 124
Criminal registers 124
Crockford's Clergy Lists 101
Cromwell, Thomas 66
Cumberland (Cumbria) 83, 156
Curia Regis Rolls 90
Customs & Excise 95,99
Customs House, Dublin 109

Darnley, Henry, King Consort of
  Scotland 15
Darwin, Charles 9, 29
Dates before 1752 77, 78
De Banco Rolls 90
Death certificate indexes 59
Declaration of Indulgence 70
Denbighshire 168
Description Books 95
Diaspora, Jewish 22
Diocesan Record Offices 66, 69
Disraeli, Benjamin 32
Dissenters 70
Divorce records 61
Domesday Book 87
Dorchester 119
Dorset 120
Drapers' Company 102
Dublin 52, 83, 108, 134, 154
Dugdale's Baronage 27
Dugdale, William 27
Duke of York's Military School 97
Dumfries & Galloway 169
Durham 23, 83
Dutch 117, 125
Dutch merchants 118
Dyfed 166

East Anglia 119
Eastern coast of America 117, 118
East India Company 103, 147
East Sussex 156
Edinburgh 52, 90, 101, 107, 134,
  154
Edward III, K. of England 14, 45
Egypt 20
Enclosure awards 88, 132
England 69, 83, 119, 121, 154
English 117
English Civil Wars 120
English merchants 118

INDEX

INDEX